THE UNIQUE PRINCESS

THE UNIQUE PRINCESS

Understanding the Significance of Modesty in Building the Jewish Home

Rabbi Yirmiyohu and Tehilla Abramov

חינוך לחיי המשפחה
Jewish Marriage Education

First Printing

Published by:
Jewish Marriage Education
P.O.B. 43206
Jerusalem 91431
www.JewishFamily.org

Printed in Israel

BS"D, Kislev 5764

After the Vaad HaRabbonim headed by Hagaon Rabbi Yitzchok Zilberstein shlita reviewed and edited the books and the full contents of the lectures of Jewish Marriage Education directed by the Abramov family - we hereby bless them that they merit to continue to spread Kedushah and Taharah within Klal Yisroel.

Yosef Sholom Elyashiv	**Aharon Y.Leib Shteinman**	**Moshe Shmuel Shapiro**	**Chaim Kanievsky**

יצחק זילברשטיין
רב שכונת רמת אלחנן
בני - ברק
וראש כולל "בית דוד" - חולון

בס"ד כו תמוז תשע"א

"ברוך אתה ה' [illegible] מלך העולם שעשני כרצונו."

מצינו בספר האדמו"ר מסטמאר זצ"ל (רבינו יואל) שביאור הברכה היא כדלהלן:

האשה מברכת את השי"ת שנתן לה אפשרות לעשות כרצונו,

כי [illegible], על הצניעות והרגשי מלכות של בנות ישראל, ומתנה

של "שרה באהל" ועל היכולת להיות "חומה לרעיה" ודוגמא

[illegible] לרעיה. ושזו לה לאשה שעושה את עצמה

רצונו, כל [illegible] בצניעותה

ספר זה "[illegible] היחודית" תרם הרבה לבנות

ישראל, לעשות רצון אבינו שבשמים

[חותמת: יצחק זילברשטיין רב שכונת רמת אלחנן בני-ברק ת"ו]

מרן הגאון רבי יוסף שלום אלישיב שליט"א:

בס"ד

אחרי שהגאון ר"י זילברשטיין שליט"א

עבר על הספר הנ"ל ומצא כי הדברים

ראויים, הנני לברך את המחבר שליט"א

כי יראו ברכה בעמלם [חתימה]

[illegible]

על הפסוק (ישעיה ס')

"אני ה' בעתה אחישנה" המדבר בענין

הגאולה העתידה. דרשו חז"ל "זכו אחישנה"

ומבאר הגר"א כי [illegible] תלוי בעיקר בשמירת הצניעות

[illegible]

[illegible]

בברכה [illegible] באהבה

שמחה הכהן [חתימה]

[חותמת: שמחה הכהן קוק רחובות רב ראשי ואב"ד]

Rabbi Yitzchak Silberstein
Rabbi of Ramat Elchanan
Bnei Brak

יצחק זילברשטיין
רב שכונת רמת אלחנן
בני - ברק
וראש כולל "בית דוד" - חולון

BS"D 26 Tammuz 5771

"Blessed are You, Hashem, our G-d, King of the universe, for having made me according to His will." I heard the following explanation of this blessing from the Satmar Rebbe, *zt"l* (Rabbeinu Yoel): A woman blesses G-d for giving her the opportunity to carry out His will, every single moment, through her modesty and the royal garments of the daughters of Israel, through conducting herself like "Sarah in her tent," and through serving as a "sturdy wall" for her husband and an example for her children, in accordance with the teaching, "Do not abandon the Torah of your mother." Praiseworthy is the woman who fashions herself "according to His will," through her modesty at all times and at every hour.

This book, *The Unique Princess*, offers a great deal to the daughters of Israel, to help them carry out the will of their Father in heaven.

Yitzchak Zilberstein

"I am G-d, in its time I will hasten it" (Yeshayahu 9). This verse speaks of the future Redemption. Our Sages have explained: "If they merit, I will hasten it." In the opinion of the Gra, this depends primarily on proper observance of the laws of modesty.

Accordingly, may the Abramov family be blessed for their blessed work, promoting the holiness of the Jewish home.

With a loving blessing of *Kohanim*,

Simcha HaCohen Kook

Aryeh Dvir

BS"D

Since HaGaon Rav Y. Zilberstein, *shlita*, has reviewed this book and deemed it appropriate and worthwhile, I offer my blessing that the authors—may they live and be well—will see blessing emerge from their labors.

Yosef Sholom Elyashiv

Rabbi CHAIM P. SCHEINBERG
Rosh Hayeshiva "TORAH ORE"
and Morah Hora'ah of Kiryat Mattersdorf

הרב חיים פינחס שיינברג
ראש ישיבת "תורה אור"
ומורה הוראה דקרית מטרסדורף

BS"D 25 Tishrei 5772

I hereby wish to strengthen HaRav Yirmiyohu Abramov, *shlita*, and his good wife, *shetichyeh*, in the activities which they have undertaken with complete dedication and without any monetary compensation, to help *klal Yisrael* conduct a Torah home—the foundation of Israel's holiness—in terms of both *halachah* and *hashkafah*.

As is well known, all of these *halachos* have been studied and tested in minute detail by the great Torah luminaries of our generation, as have the presentation of the material and the training of counselors to strengthen souls in the performance of Hashem's commandments. They are in constant consultation with outstanding Torah scholars in carrying out every detail of these activities.

Numerous homes in Eretz Yisrael, and throughout the world, have been built on holy foundations through their guidance. Directly or indirectly, they have used their wisdom to rescue many from a "*churban*," a destruction, about which it says "the altar sheds tears."

"It is worthwhile to urge only those who are already motivated." I'd like to recommend, encourage, and strengthen them, so that they may continue to tirelessly pursue their wonderful activities. And may G-d's blessing be upon you.

חיים פינחס שיינברג

Chaim Pinchas Scheinberg

OVADIA YOSSEF
RISHON LEZION
AND PRESIDENT OF TORAH SAGES COUNSIL

עובדיה יוסף
הראשון לציון
ונשיא מועצת חכמי התורה

JERUSALEM כ' כסלו תשע"ב ירושלים

מכתב ברכה

I have been shown the manuscript of the book "The Unique Princess," about modesty guidelines and the holiness of the daughters of Israel, written by Rav Yirmiyahu Abramov, shlita, and his good wife, Rebbetzin Tehilla, who have accomplished so much to fortify the walls of the Jewish home and its holiness—both through their books on the subject and through the organization, "Jewish Marriage Education," whose goal is to promote an awareness and deeper understanding of Jewish marriage and family life, in accordance with our holy Torah and the heritage that has been handed down from generation to generation.

With this book, they have merited adding another important layer of brick to the edifice of education about true modesty which unfortunately in this generation immodest dress has proliferated. This book has been reviewed and edited by renowned Torah luminaries who are well versed in these matters, to guide Jewish girls in the proper path of "All the honor of a princess lies within." It is written with intelligence and good taste: "Like golden apples carved on silver plates, so is a word spoken in its proper place." May their strength always be used for Torah and good deeds.

May they merit reciting a blessing over the completed work soon, and may their springs continue to gush forth, to elevate and strengthen the Torah, in nachas and tranquility and all good things. And may they meet with tremendous success in everything that they do.

עובדיה יוסף

Ovadia Yossef

On page 133, they write that all of a woman's hair must be covered, and that if a woman wears a wig, the wig must be a modest one, etc. They add that, in the opinion of HaGaon Rav Y. S. Elyashiv, shlita, it is preferable that hair be covered with a kerchief rather than a wig. However, see what I have written in my book of responsa, Yabia Omer, Section 4, (Even Ha'Ezer, siman 3), which states that it is forbidden to wear a wig, except in the case of a widow or divorcee in necessary circumstances such as earning a living. And see further (Ot 2), where I quote the Maharam Al-Shakar (siman 35), who writes that in places where it is customary for women to go out with the hairs at theit temples which are out of their braids and which don't stay covered, this is permitted—and many later commentaries have relied on him.

בס"ד

Rabbi Azriel Auerbach
Rabbi of "Chaniche Hayeshivot"
53 Hapisga St., Bayit Vegan, Jerusalem

הרב עזריאל אוירבאך
רב בית הכנסת "חניכי הישיבות", בית וגן
רח' הפסגה 53, בית וגן, ירושלים

BS"D

Cheshvan 5772

Blessings and shalom to the honored Abramov family. May they live and be well.

I have received and have read the manuscript on concepts and guidelines for the modesty and holiness of the Jewish woman.

The laws of modesty for the daughters of Israel have been sanctified for generations as immutable statutes. On the day the first woman was created, *HaKadosh Baruch Hu* commanded each limb of her body: "Be modest!" The Maharal, in Nesivos Olam, has written that a woman's primary reward in the World to Come will be for her modesty.

Unfortunately, in our times, the protective walls of modesty have been breached. Sadly, the assault has spread to the religious world as well, affecting clothing styles, etc. The exigencies of our time have prompted the above mentioned family to step forward to drive the lessons of *Kol kevudah bas melech penimah,* "The entire glory of a princess is inward," into the hearts of Jewish women, through a book on the Torah of modesty written with intelligence and good taste, in accordance with the teachings of our Sages and Rabbis.

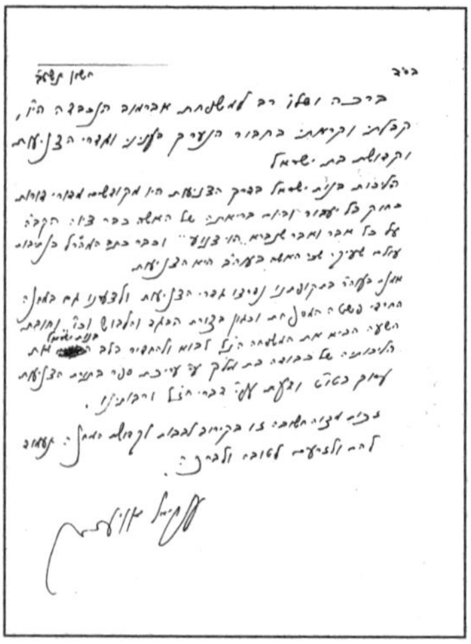

The merit of this important mitzvah of bringing hearts closer to the holiness of our people will sustain them and their descendents with goodness and blessing.

Azriel Auerbach

OHR SOMAYACH אור שמח
TANENBAUM COLLEGE

To: Rabbi Y. Abramov

The historic efforts of Rabbi Yirmeyahu and Tehillah Abramov in the field of marriage enrichment through their educational programs and literature reach a new climax with the publication of their latest work, "The Unique Princess."

In an era when the concept of *tzeniyut* is not sufficiently understood as a sacred value, this timely book written in a style which makes it interesting reading, offers a practical approach which communicates the important message of modesty as the gift of dignity.

Outstanding Torah authorities have already given their enthusiastic approval of the books which the Abramovs have written and it is a privilege to add my own recommendation along with a blessing to continue their important work for Klall Yisrael.

Mendel Weinbach

Rabbi Mendel Weinbach
Rosh Yeshivas Ohr Somayach

אשר זעליג וייס
כגן 8
פעיה"ק ירושלים ת"ו

BS"D

Date: Erev Rosh HaShanah 5772

The principle of *tzniyus*, modesty, is the most basic foundation in the purity of the Jewish home, and the reason our Sages have promised modest Jewish women outstanding blessings.

"When a woman conducts herself in accordance with *das Yehudis*, and is modest, she will merit having sons who are Torah scholars and men of good deeds, as it says, 'Your children will be like olive shoots, surrounding your table'" (*Bamidbar Rabbah* 8).

This marvelous book, which has received the blessing of the *gadol hador*, Maran Rabbeinu HaGaon Rav Yosef Sholom Elyashiv, *shlita*, was written with the aim of implanting and explaining to Jewish girls the beauty of this wonderful trait of modesty.

My blessings to HaRav Abramov, *shlita*, and his rebbetzin, *tichyeh*, that through them there will be an increase of holiness in Israel.

With a blessing for a *kesivah v'chasimah tovah*,
and with the honor of the Torah,

הן מדת הצניעות היא יסוד היסודות דקדושת הבית היהודי, ולא בכדי הבטיחו חז"ל לנשים הצנועות בישראל ברכה מופלגת.

"בזמן שהאשה נוהגת בעצמה דת יהודית והיא צנועה, זוכה שיצאו ממנה בנים בעלי מקרא, בעלי משנה, בעלי מעשים טובים, שנאמר בניך כשתילי זיתים" (במ"ר ח').

ספר נפלא זה שקיבל את ברכת גדול הדור מרן רבינו הגרי"ש אלישיב שליט"א, מטרתו להחדיר ולהסביר לבנות ישראל את יופיה של מדה מופלאה זו הצניעות.

ברכתי להרב אברמוב שליט"א ורעייתו תחי' שעל ידם תרבה הקדושה בישראל.

בברכת כוח"ט
ובכבוד התורה

אשר זעליג וייס
אב"ד וראש ישיבת "דרכי תורה"
פעיה"ק ירושלים ת"ו

Asher Zelig Weiss
Av Beis Din and Rosh
Yeshivas Darchei Torah

בס"ד

משה מרדכי קארפ
קרית ספר

7 Cheshvan 5772

This book, *The Unique Princess*, on matters of modesty, which has earned the approbation of Rabbeinu Maran Rav Y. S. Elyashiv, *shlita*, and has been reviewed by *gedolei Torah*, is urgently needed in our generation, in which concepts and values that were so holy and so simple in previous generations have been distorted through the curses of *ikvasa d'Meshicha* into the category of "rampaging wickedness." To that end, my friend Rabbi Yirmiyohu Abramov, *shlita*, and his good wife, *tichyeh*, have undertaken to write this book, in order to transmit the values of modesty and holiness to the daughters of Israel in an easy-to-read language and in a style that is suitable also for those who have been open to today's modern influences. This book is of great benefit to bring the light of modesty to every Jewish home. Therefore, my blessing to those who have brought this book to fruition, that they may merit to spread the light of modesty and holiness in Israel. And may it be His will that, in the merit of righteous women who will strengthen themselves in these matters and in the framework of holiness, we will all merit hastening the Redemption, speedily in our days, amein.

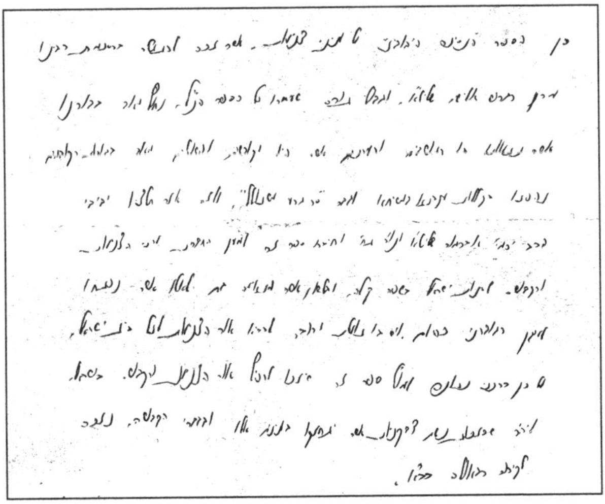

Moshe Mordechai Karp

בס"ד

Rabbi Zev Leff

Rabbi of Moshav Matityahu
Rosh HaYeshiva—Yeshiva Gedola Matityahu

הרב זאב לף

מרא דאתרא מושב מתתיהו
ראש הישיבה—ישיבה גדולה מתתיהו

D.N. Modiin 71917 | Tel: 08-976-1138 טל' | Fax: 08-976-5326 פקס' | ד.נ. מודיעין 71917

Dear Friends,

My first thought was to be skeptical if there is any place for me to write an approbation to the book "The Unique Princess" since greater individuals than myself, first and foremost Maran HaRav HaGaon Rav Yosef Sholom Eliyashev, have already given their approbations. But, after some contemplation I feel that my approbation is in place in order that people not mistakenly feel that the contents of this book are meant only for great and spiritually lofty individuals and that its contents are things beyond the letter of the law and matters of extra piety. Such is not the case, each and every Jew is a prince and princess, children of the king of kings, a member of the kingdom of Kohanim and a holy nation. Hence all the topics of tznius presented in this work in such a clear and interesting manner, both hashkafah and halachah are outlooks and laws that apply to everyone even regular people as ourselves.

I appreciate the tremendous effort put into producing this magnificent presentation and I commend Rabbi and Mrs. Yirmiyahu Abramov for this accomplishment.

I hope they will see great satisfaction insofar that this book will be disseminated and received well in Klal Yisroel and make an impression and improvement in that which Hashem requests of us, "To walk modestly with our G-d."

Sincerely,
With Torah blessings

Rabbi Zev Leff

Rebbetzin B. Kanievsky

BS"D 7 Tishrei 5772

Terrible trouble has been thrust upon the Jewish people in recent years: indescribable tragedies of widows and orphans.

Our great rabbis were asked why this is happening and what can be done to repair matters. The rabbis have answered that it is because of a lack of modesty, and that this matter must be repaired quickly. They suggested that each and every woman take upon herself some improvement in this area.

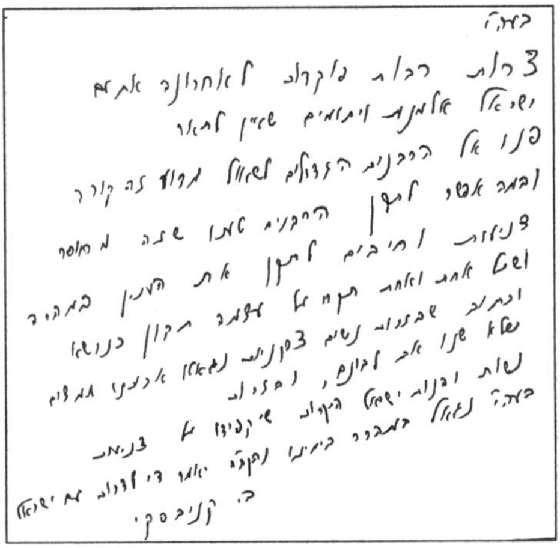

בס"ד

צרות רבות נוקדו לאחרונה את עם
ישראל אלמנות ויתומים שאין לתאר
פנו אל הרבנים הגדולים לשאול מדוע זה קורה
ובמה אפשר לתקן הרבנים ענו שזה מחוסר
צניעות וחייבים לתקן את הענין במהירה
ושכל אחת ואחת תקח על עצמה תקון בצניעות
ונכתב שבזכות נשים צדקניות נגאלו אבותינו ממצרים
שלא שנו את לבושם, ובזכות
נשות ובנות ישראל היקרות שיקפידו על צניעות
בעזה"י נגאל במהרה בימינו והקב"ה יאמר די לצרות של ישראל
ב. קניבסקי

It is written that we were redeemed from Egypt in the merit of the righteous women who did not change the way they dressed and in the merit of dear Jewish women and girls who will be careful about their modesty, with G-d's help we will be redeemed speedily in our days, and *HaKadosh Baruch Hu* will say "Enough!" to the suffering of the nation of Israel.

B. Kanievsky

In memory of the Righteous Rebbetzin

לעילוי נשמת הרבנית הצדקנית

מרת **בת שבע אסתר קניבסקי** ע"ה

בת מרן הגאון רבי יוסף שלום אלישיב שליט"א

אשת הגאון הגדול רבי חיים קניבסקי שליט"א

נלב"ע י"ז בתשרי תשע"ב

ת.נ.צ.ב.ה.

Our Thanks To –

- HaGaon HaRav Avraham Chaim Feuer, *shlita*, for allowing us to use the ideas that he presented in his lecture on the mitzvah of head-covering.
- Mrs. Miriam Jacubowicz, *tichyeh*, whose creative writing skills have enabled this book to emerge.
- Mrs. Rina Shachar, *tichyeh*, who put great effort into the translation of the book into Hebrew.
- Mrs. Ronit Ben-David, *tichyeh*, and Mrs. Leah Geliss, *tichyeh*, for their warm and professional editing of the Hebrew book.
- Mrs. Libby Lazewnik, *tichyeh*, for the great effort she put into the translation from the Hebrew.
- Mrs. Ita Olesker, *tichyeh*, for her excellent editing of the English book.
- Mrs. Gittel Kaplan, *tichyeh,* for her devoted efforts in preparing this book for print.
- All those whose encouragement was the force which made this book a reality.
- May we merit that all Jewish home be built in holiness and purity, and peace should reign therein. "So that we, and our descendants of all of *Am Yisrael* should all know Your Name and learn Your Torah..." (from *Tefillas HaShelah*).
- May we merit the complete redemption with the coming of *Moshiach Tzidkeinu*, speedily in our days.

With heartfelt praise and gratitude to *Hashem Yisborach,*
Yirmiyohu and Tehilla Abramov

In memory of our dear parents
לעילוי נשמות הורינו היקרים

My mother, my teacher
מרת חסיה ב"ר אברהם איסר
אברמוב ע"ה
נלב"ע ב' בתשרי תשנ"ב
ת.נ.צ.ב.ה.

My father, my teacher
ר' אוריאל חיים ב"ר ישראל
אברמוב ז"ל
נלב"ע ב' בניסן תשכ"ד
ת.נ.צ.ב.ה.

My mother, my teacher
מרת רבקה ב"ר שלום
כץ ע"ה
נלב"ע ז' במנחם אב תש"ס
ת.נ.צ.ב.ה.

My father, my teacher
ר' ישראל אלכסנדר ב"ר חיים בן-ציון
כץ ז"ל
נלב"ע ט"ו באדר תשמ"ה
ת.נ.צ.ב.ה.

In memory of our dear grandparents
לעילוי נשמות זקנינו היקרים

ר' אברהם איסר ב"ר דוד שלמה
שלומוביץ ז"ל
נלב"ע ה' באדר ראשון תש"ו
ת.נ.צ.ב.ה.

ר' ישראל ב"ר אברהם
אברמוב ז"ל
נלב"ע כ"ז באדר תרצ"ז
ת.נ.צ.ב.ה.

מרת שרה ב"ר משה
שלומוביץ ע"ה
נלב"ע א' במנחם אב תשי"ב
ת.נ.צ.ב.ה.

מרת דבורה ב"ר שלמה
אברמוב ע"ה
נלב"ע י' בתשרי תשי"ד
ת.נ.צ.ב.ה.

ר' שלום ב"ר צבי
אסטרוף ז"ל
נלב"ע כ"ג בשבט תש"ז
ת.נ.צ.ב.ה.

ר' חיים בן-ציון ב"ר שלום
כץ הי"ד
נלב"ע בחורבן אירופה
ת.נ.צ.ב.ה.

מרת רחל פרידא ב"ר אבא נתן
אוסטרוף ע"ה
נלב"ע כ"ח בניסן תשל"ח
ת.נ.צ.ב.ה.

מרת רחל גליקא ב"ר שמואל
כץ הי"ד
נלב"ע בחורבן אירופה
ת.נ.צ.ב.ה.

In memory of our dear teacher

לעילוי נשמת רבנו מורה דרכנו

מרן הגאון

רבי שלמה זלמן אויערבאך זצוק"ל

נלב"ע כ' באדר ראשון תשנ"ה

ת.נ.צ.ב.ה.

Contents

Introduction 21
Chapter 1: Modesty and the World 24
Chapter 2: The World's Influence 31
Chapter 3: A Woman's Strength 39
Chapter 4: Recognizing the Challenge 46
Chapter 5: Understanding the Solution 53
Chapter 6: Practically Speaking 58
Chapter 7: Modesty and Marriage 65
Chapter 8: Hair and Imagination 74
Chapter 9: Royal Crown 86
Chapter 10: The Additional Challenge 98
Chapter 11: Especially for Husbands 112
Chapter 12: Summary of the Laws of *Yichud* 123
Chapter 13: The Engaged Couple 127
Chapter 14: The Laws of Modesty 133
Chapter 15: A G-d-Fearing Woman, She Shall Be Praised 146
Modesty Enrichment Material:
HaGaon HaRav Yitzchak Zilberstein 159

Introduction

As she presented a last few stimulating thoughts and wound down her lecture, Mrs. Fine gazed out at the crowd of women who had come to hear her speak. She was a dynamic speaker who was able to attract many to her lectures. The auditorium was packed with women of all ages who clearly did not belong to the city's Orthodox community. Perhaps, she hoped fervently, she'd be able to draw them closer to a life of Torah and mitzvos.

Tonight's subject had been titled "The True Essence and Dignity of the Jewish Woman." Mrs. Fine finished speaking and looked around. "Questions?" she asked, opening up the floor. Eager hands went up. She called on a young woman sitting at the back of the hall.

"Please go ahead," Mrs. Fine said with an encouraging smile.

"This was a fascinating lecture," the young woman began. "But, to be very honest, I don't understand how your description of the Jewish woman as a princess whose dignity comes from within—as you quoted, 'a princess whose glory is inward'—compares with many of the religious women whom I see on the streets. With their long, gorgeous wigs blowing in

the breeze and snug clothing that shows off their figures, they don't seem to me to be the epitome of the dignified Jewish princess!"

Mrs. Fine's mouth went dry. What could she answer? "Please, Hashem," she prayed silently, "help me. Put the right words in my mouth."

Suddenly she had a brainstorm. Honesty is the best policy, she told herself. There was no point in trying to camouflage the truth. She took a deep breath, and murmured another fervent prayer before she began.

"Thank you for your question," she said. "It is certainly one that needs to be asked.

"In fact, there is a great deal of confusion in the area of proper dress and appearance. Women don't always know how to draw the fine line between what is appropriate and what is inappropriate, in terms of both dress and conduct. Just last week, I personally attended an evening devoted to improving modesty within the Torah-observant community. We heard lectures from well-known rabbis and were given pamphlets with detailed guidelines for wigs and clothes that adhere to the most comprehensive laws of modesty. So, you see, even women who are fully observant must constantly keep learning how to live up to their princess status. Unfortunately, many of them are completely unaware that their attire is unsuitable.

"Let me add something personal. Recently, when I had my own wig redone according to these guidelines, and when I went through my wardrobe once again to remove any halachically borderline items, I felt exalted. I too am trying to improve. Modesty is a lifetime journey. The more deeply we understand our feminine essence, the easier it will be for us to grow in this area."

With a smile, Mrs. Fine concluded her answer and accepted a question from another woman in the hall. She knew, though, that the first question posed to her that evening would stay with her for a long time.

In fact, it just might stay with her forever.

Chapter 1

Modesty and the World

Never in the history of mankind has there been such an exposed generation. Today's society knows no boundaries. Virtually everything that is meant to be hidden and private has become exposed and public—to the extent that this exposure has become a symbol of our times.

People of all ages walk around in public improperly dressed, without feeling the slightest shame or compunction about it. Society has ceased to feel a natural embarrassment about the idea of excessive exposure, completely unaware of the ugliness and the moral flaw inherent in this.

How, we ask ourselves, has this impossible reality become possible?

While it is true that most people don't give much thought to their manner of dress—or, more accurately, the lack thereof—

and simply follow the dictates of contemporary fashion, there is a deeper reason for this phenomenon. The reason is rooted in a lack of belief in a Creator. This idea is expressed by Rav Yitzchak Hutner, *zt"l*: "There is a vast difference between the nightmarish immodesty confronting us today and manifestations of immodesty that appeared in previous times. Today's immodesty does not constitute a simple stumbling or straying.... On the contrary, it is nothing but a rebellion against the principles of faith—which are found in the essence of modesty—and an uprising against any sort of exalted view in life" (*Pachad Yitzchak*, letter 49).

In a similar vein, Rav Eliyohu Lopian, *zt"l*, writes: "Because of our many sins, a plague of public licentiousness and immodesty has erupted in our time. An atmosphere of debauchery and wantonness whose source is heresy, a denial of *Hashem Yisbarach* and His Torah, runs rampant, casting young and old, children and women, into the depths, *r"l*. The sinners have poisoned the air, making the heart foolish and rotten, so that everyone must be wary lest he too be tainted with this sickness, Heaven forbid..." (*Lev Eliyahu*, vol. 1, p. 37; vol. 2, p. 236).

When a person denies, Heaven forbid, the existence of the Creator, then he comes to see himself as nothing more than a sophisticated animal. Coming from this perspective, it follows that he—like the apes whom he believes to be his ancestors—requires little clothing.

> *Maran HaGaon Rav Yaakov Kamenetsky, zt"l, rosh yeshivah of Torah Vodaas, was once traveling on an airplane going from the US to Israel along with several of his grandchildren. From time to time over the course of the flight, the grandchildren would come over to Rav Yaakov and respectfully see to his every need. They accorded their illustrious grandfather the reverence that he deserved, as one of the greatest roshei yeshivah in the last generation.*

On the same flight, near Rav Kamenetsky's seat, sat a well-known personality, then serving as head of the Histadrut worker's union. He observed the spectacle with astonishment and envy.

Toward the end of the trip, he could not keep silent any longer. Approaching the rosh yeshivah, he asked, "How is it that your grandchildren show you such incredible respect? I too have children and grandchildren, but not one of them treats me that way. Can you tell me your secret?"

With a compassionate look in his eye, Rav Yaakov replied, "The Jewish people, who follow the ways of the Torah transmitted to us at Sinai, know how to recognize and appreciate the greatness of those who came before them." The rosh yeshivah went on to describe the chain of Jewish generations, era after era.

"The further away a generation is from the glory of those who lived previously, the relatively more diminished it becomes. This is why my grandchildren respect their grandfather, who came two generations before them and who saw, with his own eyes, men of great Torah and piety who sat in the dust of the giants who came before them.

"Your own worldview is the polar opposite. Young people look down with scorn on those who are older than they are, and they believe that older people don't reach their ankles! After all, they—the young ones—have become more 'sophisticated' than their parents, thanks to advancing scientific knowledge. On what basis would you wish your children to accord respect to the generation that came before them?"

(As told by Rabbi Yitzchak Zilberstein, shlita)

"Man is the glory of G-d; the glory of man is his garments" (*Derech Eretz Zutah* 10). As believing Jews, we know that man was created in the image of G-d, therefore he is a unique and superior being. As such, he possesses deep within him the fundamental trait of shame, which is a prerequisite of modesty. Women, in particular, were created with this trait, as G-d formed them from the rib—a part of man that is concealed.

"When G-d created woman, he contemplated from where to create her, a hidden place in man.... And as He formed each of her limbs, He commanded her, 'Be a modest woman, be a modest woman...'" (*Bereishis Rabbah* 18:2). Unfortunately, in the bitter and painful reality of our times, many women are in a hurry to discard this exalted trait. The stores are full of immodest clothing for sale, and women are buying and wearing them despite the fact that they contradict their essential nature. Initially, a woman may feel uncomfortable in such scanty clothing that doesn't cover her properly. But with the human tendency to "go with the flow" of prevailing social trends, she will soon overcome her discomfort and grow accustomed to it. All too soon, she loses her sensitivity and no longer gives a second thought to her undignified appearance.

There are, however, tools that we human beings can utilize to help us hold onto our natural human sensitivity in this area. We must use these tools, and not let ourselves be dragged along after passing fashions.

The current situation is an insult and an embarrassment to us all. All of humanity is descended from the first man, Adam, who was given that name because he was created in the image of G-d—as it says, "So G-d created man in His image, in the image of G-d He created him" (Bereishis 1:27). In the Midrash, Rabbi Meir likens man's image to that of his Creator, in that G-d, Himself, gave Adam and Chava garments and dressed them in "a garment of light" (*Bereishis Rabbah* 20:29). It is said of G-d that He "covers with light," as with a garment (Tehillim 104:2).

The Shelah HaKadosh, in his *Toldos Adam* (third introduction), writes: "If he clings to G-d and tries to resemble Him by walking in His ways, his name will be, in essence, 'Adam,' from the term, *adameh l'elyon,* 'I will liken myself to the Most High' (Yeshayahu 14:14)…. Indeed, man's name, with its connotation of resemblance to the One above, reflects his essential purpose."

Thus, every human being has a natural and inborn sensitivity to modesty. How much more so does our nation, the Chosen People, excel in this trait! "Just as a dove is modest, so too Israel is modest" (*Shir HaShirim Rabbah* 1:63). Jewish women, in particular, are rewarded for developing this virtue. "The trait of modesty is extremely praiseworthy, and especially so in women" (HaMeiri, *Yoma* 47a). "The primary praise of a woman and her high spiritual level is her modesty" (*Kisvei HaMaharal*, vol. 2, p. 340).

Rav Moshe Feinstein, *zt"l*, explains that even though the main concept of modesty is modesty in front of other people, the concept is also expressed between man and G-d: "For the sake of Heaven's honor, as 'the whole world is filled with His glory,'" and also between man and himself: "The concept of modesty applies even with respect to an individual himself—perhaps to train himself to modesty" (*Iggrot Moshe, Yoreh Deah*, vol. 3, p. 283).

Rabbi Yitzchak of Corbeil includes the commandment to be modest in the count of the mitzvos: "To be modest, as it says: 'So your camp shall be holy' (Devarim 23:15), as it is written, 'Walk modestly with your G-d' (Michah 6:8)—one must behave modestly and not with licentiousness in everything" (*Semak*, mitzvah 57).

One consequence of the lack of shame in the world is an ever-growing insolence. We are living in times that the Ponovezher Rav, Rav Yosef Shlomo Kahaneman, *zt"l*, labeled *ikvasa d'Meshicha*—an era in which we hear the footsteps of the Mashiach. Throughout the long years of exile, Jews have prayed, waited, and longed for the Mashiach's arrival. And we are the generation that has been chosen to live at a time when we can already hear his footsteps approaching.

Our Sages (*Sotah* 49b) give us a detailed description of the world in the generation preceding the Mashiach:

"In the period that will precede the coming of Mashiach, insolence will increase, and costs will soar. The vine will yield its fruit yet wine will be dear, and the government will turn to heresy, and there shall be no rebuke. The [erstwhile] meeting place [of Sages] will be [used] for harlotry and the Galilee will be destroyed and the Gavlan desolated, and the people [who dwell] on the borders will wander about from town to town, but they will not be succored. And the wisdom of the scribes will decay, and those who dread sin will be despised, and truth will be absent. Youth will blanch the faces of elders; elders will stand in the presence of minors. The son derides his father; a daughter rises against her mother [and] a daughter-in-law against her mother-in-law; a man's enemies are the people of his household. The face of the generation is like the face of the dog; a son is not abashed [in the presence] of his father. Upon what, then, can we lean? Upon our Father in Heaven!"

First and foremost, our Sages tell us, insolence will strengthen and proliferate. Indeed, *chutzpah* is the outstanding feature of our time. It is accompanied by a host of other distressing phenomena, which our Sages describe as if they were living among us to witness them in person. It is obvious to anyone that immodesty emerges directly from insolence (*Chovos HaLevavos, Sha'ar HaBechinah*, ch. 5).

The most widespread and accepted practice of them all is that of children rising up against their parents, backed by so-called professionals who absolve them of any shred of blame. They are encouraged to lay the blame for all their own problems and shortcomings at their parents' door. Such conduct is the height of insolence and ingratitude, and contradicts the Jewish concepts of Divine Providence and free will. A person is ultimately responsible for his actions, and cannot blame others for his own omissions. Moreover, such blame-laying constitutes a complete negation of the commandment to honor and revere our parents and teachers. Both insolence and immodesty stem from a lack of self-respect as well as a glaring lack of respect for others and for the Creator. This has a direct causal effect on the breakup of families.

What does G-d ask from us at times like these?

Those of us who have been privileged to survive and who are Torah- and mitzvah-observant Jews, have a mission: to spread the light to the nations. "For you are a holy people to Hashem, your G-d; Hashem, your G-d, has chosen you to be for Him a treasured people above all the peoples that are on the face of the earth" (Devarim 7:6). We must become keenly aware that we have the capacity to influence the world around us. Now, more than ever, we must stand upright, strong, and respectful, and serve as models of modesty. We must fulfill our mission as representatives of a trait that is both so natural and so much to be admired: shame. A trait which today's world has disgracefully trampled beneath its arrogant foot.

The Chofetz Chaim, *zt"l*, wrote the following: "At the end of the exile, where we are today, there exists a very terrible war between purity and impurity; and impurity has thrown some devastating arrows.... Only the few have emerged from the battle with all their limbs intact. These are the survivors upon whom G-d has called. These are the true heroes. They are the people of the Torah.... Each person, on his level, encourages other servants to faithfully carry out His work..." (Chofetz Chaim on *Nach*).

Certainly, we have a great deal to be happy about. After everything that the Jewish people have endured over more than two thousand years of persecution, we are still here, and loyal to our national heritage. But it is not enough. We must strive to emulate our holy forefathers in every area of our lives.

This is no simple feat. With modesty in the world at its lowest ebb ever, how can we actualize this mission with strength and confidence?

Chapter 2

The World's Influence

The Torah advises us to know our enemy. As the Ramchal says: "It requires great astuteness and attentiveness to avoid the snares of the *yetzer* and escape evil, in order that it has no hold over us to intrude upon our deeds" (*Mesillas Yesharim* 6). If we wish to succeed in our mission and preserve our uniqueness, it is incumbent upon us to be alert to the dangers lying in ambush for us, so that we can most efficiently protect ourselves.

Let us, therefore, take a quick look at the current state of family life in the world. Reports by the National Center for Health and Statistics in the US reflect the fact that only 56% of adults in this country are married. Divorce is estimated to have tripled in the past three decades. A full 28% of American children are growing up in single-parent homes. Less than 50% of all children spend their entire childhood in an intact family unit. In practical terms, it seems as though "family" is a concept that has been lost to the world, Heaven forbid!

The consequences of these statistics for the future are alarming: many children from broken homes grow up into adults who find it hard to develop close relationships with others, to sustain stable marriages, or hold down a job for long. No one disputes the fact that the tragedy striking at the heart of the family system is exacting its toll, both physically and emotionally. People are walking around in pain, families are suffering, and children are paying the price for their parents' confusion.

Researchers agree on the strong correlation between the high divorce rate and the prevalence of every conceivable social problem.

What is the link between the dissolution of the family and the lack of modesty? Contemporary life is based on an ostentatious lifestyle and envy, both of which are hallmarks of immodesty. In contrast, the Jewish people have always been a model of the concept of modesty implied by the verse "He saw that their tent openings did not face one another" (*Rashi*, Bamidbar 24:5). The permissiveness in the society around us presents a variety of temptations, which form a formidable obstacle to the unity of the family.

What does all this have to do with us Torah-observant Jews? After all, we lead sheltered lives in our own thriving communities!

These facts certainly do affect us. Try as we might to protect ourselves, what happens in the general society does affect the religious community. Our eyes function as cameras, photographing everything they see. Our ears function as recorders, recording everything they hear. Our brains serve as sophisticated computers, storing every bit of information they absorb, like "a cemented cistern that loses not a drop" (*Avos* 2). Everything that we see and hear is etched on our souls. Just as we make sure that every bite of food we eat is *kosher*, so must we do the same to ensure the "*kashruth*" of everything that we see and hear.

There are those who claim, "I can see or hear anything without being influenced." The truth of such a claim parallels the "truth" of the claim "I can take powerful drugs without being influenced." First and foremost, we must be cognizant of the powerful influence of our surroundings. After that, we can tackle the next step: figuring out how to preserve and protect ourselves from that influence.

Rabbi Simcha Wasserman, *zt"l*, used to say that the biggest challenge our generation faces is defending ourselves against the insidious trespass of the outside world into our inner reality. Sophisticated modern technology brings the external world right into our homes, minds, and souls with the pressing of a single button. Radio, television, video, Internet, newspapers, magazines, books, and advertisements have become so readily available and accessible that only a constant alertness to the gravity of the danger can help us be wise enough to protect our souls. Negative materials enter our homes from many different directions—sometimes in a most innocent guise.

> *Rebbetzin Cohen was peeling potatoes in her kitchen on a Friday morning, when the phone rang. At the other end of the line, she heard a young woman emitting heartbreaking wails. Amid a storm of tears, she told the rebbetzin that the night before, she'd woken up to find her husband seated in front of the computer which she uses for her work, viewing despicable material. What should she do? She asked as she wept. She would never be able to forgive her husband. Their marriage, it seemed, had been destroyed overnight.*
>
> *"You use unfiltered Internet?" Rebbetzin Cohen asked in astonishment. "The rabbis have stated categorically that such a thing is forbidden! Didn't you know that?"*
>
> *"I did know," came the regretful reply. "But I thought this instruction didn't apply to us. Who would have dreamed that such a thing could happen in our good, strong home?"*

This, then, is the challenge of our times: to distance ourselves from the influences that ambush us at every turn. It is not an easy challenge at all. Our Sages, the Amoraim, said of our times, the era of *ikvasa d'Meshicha*, "*Yesei v'lo achminiah*—Let these days come, but do not let us be there to see them" (*Sanhedrin* 98b). In other words, we long for that era to arrive, but do not wish to witness the monumental challenges it will bring in its trail! As Rav Dessler, *zt"l*, explains: As the future Redemption approaches, "[the Jewish people] will have to contend with the mighty challenges that the Amoraim were afraid of when they said, '*Yesei v'lo achminiah*'.... The Maharal explained, lest they fail to withstand the test of that time" (*Michtav MeEliyahu*, vol. 2, p. 34).

If our Sages were worried that they'd be unable to withstand the ordeals of the pre-Messianic era, what are we, so greatly their inferiors, to think? How can we possibly meet these challenges?

The answer is that despite the enormous difficulty, the very fact that we are the ones forced to contend with these challenges is proof that we will also be able to triumph over them. It is a well-known principle that G-d never gives an individual a test that he or she is incapable of passing. The same principle applies to an entire generation. "*HaKadosh Baruch Hu* does not come with complaints against His people" (*Avodah Zarah* 3a). All generations inherited the spiritual genes of Avraham HaIvri, who was called this because all the world stood on one side while he stood on the other side. His descendants, the Jewish people, have been graced with the ability to withstand societal pressures. We have an innate knowledge and belief that we have the strength to meet the challenge—and, with Heaven's help, we will do so. We will choose *not* to be influenced.

To this end, we've been given clear halachic guidelines. And for this purpose, every generation has been blessed with towering Torah luminaries from whose teachings we must not deviate. By adhering to these halachic guidelines and listening to the instructions of *gedolei Yisrael* – the rabbinical leaders of our generation – we acquire clear boundaries that prevent the encroachment of insidious influences.

Malki went shopping for a new outfit in honor of the approaching holiday. One store caught her eye with a huge, colorful sign: "Sale! Everything in the store—50% off!"

Malki entered the shop and began looking at the suits and dresses hanging on the racks. Suddenly, she saw it.

Malki was enchanted. The dress was in her favorite style and a perfect color. Tomorrow morning, she'd be able to recite the blessing "Who clothes the naked" with complete sincerity over this outfit, she thought happily. Holding her breath, she took the outfit off its hanger. She already knew she'd look wonderful in it. She tried the outfit on and gazed at her reflection in the mirror to measure the fit. Just beautiful, she thought with satisfaction.... But wait a minute. Was the skirt a bit shorter than the permitted length, or was that just her imagination?

"You look glorious!" cried a saleswoman, hurrying over to her. "Just look at the way the color matches your eyes! I'm sure you've noticed that the make is one of the best. And today, you can buy it at a 50% discount off the original price! You didn't even have to try it on—it's obviously a perfect fit. Shall I wrap it up for you?"

"Just one minute," Malki said hesitantly. "I'm not quite sure about the length."

The saleswoman stepped back and studied the skirt. "No problem! It covers your knees with room to spare," she reassured her customer with confidence.

"I want to make sure it's halachically long enough," Malki said firmly.

"Certainly." The saleswoman smiled. There was no chance in the world that this customer would pass up such a bargain. She was sure of it. She went to get a measuring tape and began measuring the skirt length. Both she and Malki held their breath hoping that it would be okay.

Finally, the saleswoman straightened up with a satisfied smile.

"Perfect!" she announced triumphantly. "This skirt is only two centimeters shorter than the one you're wearing now."

"Thank you for all your effort," Malki said with decision. "But I won't buy a skirt that's shorter than the halachic requirement—even if only by two centimeters."

Hanging the outfit back on the rack, she walked out of the store, leaving behind a stunned saleswoman still holding the tape measure in her hand. Though she'd just lost a profitable sale, she could not help but admire a Jewish woman who was able to be unwaveringly loyal to the parameters of Jewish law.

Modesty protects that which is most precious to us. Our task is to accurately gauge its value to us, so that we will have the necessary willpower to withstand alien influences. As the Chofetz Chaim used to say: "The apple doesn't fall far from the tree—but this is only true when there are no strong winds blowing in the area." Today, as we all know, there are very strong winds out there.

The first thing we must understand is the consequence of even the slightest deviation from that which is permissible. Where could a mere two centimeters take us?

It was a tense moment on the launching pad. The spaceship was about to be launched into outer space—destination: Mars! The countdown began.

"Ten…nine…eight…seven…"

The anticipation in the air was palpable.

"Four…three…two…"

Suddenly, at the crucial instant, the countdown broke off. The launch had been aborted! After all the prolonged and feverish preparations, the rocket would not be launched to Mars after all.

"What happened?" cried all of those present. "What went wrong?"

The head NASA scientist hastened to explain. "The spaceship was a quarter-millionth of an inch off its bearings. We had no choice but to cancel the launch!"

"Are you people insane?" the civilians asked incredulously. "For a mere quarter-millionth of an inch, you abort a launch? The cancellation of this project will cost 27 million dollars! What a waste of the taxpayers' money!"

The scientist smiled, and waved a dismissive hand. "You civilians, who have no notion of the basic principles of astronomy, simply do not understand. Had we ignored the deviation of a quarter-millionth of an inch, this rocket would never have reached Mars. Who knows? It might have reached Jupiter instead! A deviation of a quarter-millionth of an inch at the start of the journey translates into an enormous deviation by the end of it!"

We must be aware of the dangers inherent in even the slightest deviation from the correct path. Ignoring a gap of two centimeters in length, or exposing a tiny bit of elbow or knee, may seem harmless. In actuality, however, its potential for damage is very great.

First, it is a breach of obedience to halachic guidelines—a grave matter in and of itself. In addition, with the passage of time and the march of the generations, a tiny deviation like this can widen into a breach of mammoth proportions. Many, many of our fellow Jews have fallen victim to such tiny deviations. The breakup of the family unit and the high rate of intermarriage are two painful examples of where one may wind up at the end of the road.

Sometimes it all starts with one small compromise. Two centimeters become four, and then six, then eight, and so on. From there, it's only a short step to deviating from the halachah in other areas—a deviation whose end point one can only guess.

Being aware of the danger of tiny deviations is a big part of the battle. The second part is simply learning how to avoid the pitfalls. G-d has given us the key: "Only beware for yourself and greatly beware for your soul" (Devarim 4:9). Rabbi Shimshon Raphael Hirsch explains this verse very simply: Stay away from foreign influences, because foreign thoughts remove Torah from the heart.

"But you, who cling to Hashem, your G-d—you are all alive today" (Devarim 4:4). We are a nation that clings to *HaKadosh Baruch Hu*. Every Jew must focus constantly on the mission that G-d has placed upon him: "You shall be to Me a kingdom of priests and a holy nation" (Shemos 19:6); "[They] shall say, 'Surely a wise and discerning people is this great nation!'" (Devarim 4:6). Being the nation whose mission it is to show the way to the rest of the world, surely we would not dream of learning from the ways of the nations of the world and imitating them.

The exile in which we find ourselves today, *galus Edom,* is characterized by emptiness. Eisav, father of Edom, had nothing better to do with his time than hunt animals. This emptiness led to licentiousness and corruption of character. Our challenge is to make sure that no vestige of Edom's influence clings to us: neither their streets, their fashions, their media , their values, their materialism, their manner of speaking, their conduct—in short, their emptiness. This is our test and our challenge. The words *nisayon*, "test" and *nes*, "miracle" come from the same root. Both express elevation and exaltation.

From where are we to draw the strength to elevate ourselves and stand up to this test and this challenge, meted out to us by G-d Himself?

Chapter 3

A Woman's Strength

Mazel tov! The grandson of a great Chassidic rebbe had just become engaged to the daughter of an illustrious Litvishe rosh yeshivah. Important figures from across the Jewish spectrum had been invited to attend the engagement celebration.

Rav Yechezkel Sarne, rosh yeshivah of the Chevron Yeshivah and a wise and clever man, posed a riddle to the group of Torah luminaries who graced the happy event.

"Who is the person that has had the greatest impact on the Jewish people in the last hundred years?" Rav Sarne asked.

Each of those present was certain that the person in question must be one of his own illustrious forebears. The roshei yeshivah were sure that it was one of the famous heads of the great Lithuanian yeshivahs, while the scions of the various Chassidic dynasties believed that the person must be a previous Chassidic rebbe.

"No," said Rav Sarne. "This person is not from any of your families."

The guests were stunned. No one could venture a guess at who Rav Sarne was referring to.

"Let me give you another hint," Rav Sarne continued. "The person in question never learned a single page of Gemara!"

His audience was now totally confused. How was it possible that someone who'd wielded such enormous influence on the Jewish people had never even cracked open a Gemara?

"And not only that," Rav Sarne went on with complete confidence, "but when I tell you who it is, you will all agree with me!"

And so it was. When he revealed that the name of the person he had in mind was Sarah Schenirer, one and all agreed that he was correct.

Sarah Schenirer was a seamstress in Cracow, Poland. The Jewish women and girls who ordered dresses from her wanted them to be sewn in accordance with the fashions prevalent at the time. The mode of her customers' dress so pained her that she often dampened the cloth she was sewing with her tears.

But she didn't leave it at that. Sarah Schenirer had the courage to fix the situation. She set out to raise the spiritual level of the Jewish girls.

Despite the formidable obstacles that blocked her way, she went on to establish the Bais Yaakov movement. Under her guidance, girls grew up with the desire and suitability to marry yeshivah students whose lives were dedicated to the study of Torah.

Rabbi Moshe Yechiel Skozialitz was one of the human skeletons that the Nazis put to work in one of their forced-labor camps. One day, a group of laborers was given the terrible job of laying railroad tracks across the site of a Jewish cemetery. The poor unfortunates were ordered to uproot the tombstones of their dear ones who were buried there. There are no words to describe their anguish.

The workers were given large sledgehammers and told to demolish the tombstones with them. A sharp pain pierced Rabbi Moshe Yechiel's heart each time he struck a stone and watched the fragments scatter in every direction, taking away with them the memory of another precious Jew. In the course of his work, he came to a certain tombstone that refused to shatter under the force of his blows. Knowing that his life depended on it, he raised the sledgehammer and lowered it with all his might on the stone. It stood firm.

The Nazi who was supervising the group saw what was happening and stalked over. "I'll show you how to do it right!" he snarled, punctuating his remark with a few well-aimed kicks and curses. The soldier picked up the sledgehammer and brought it down with every ounce of his strength. The tombstone didn't budge. Instead, the sledgehammer's heavy metal head became detached and flew off.

The Nazi, who'd lost face in front of his group, left the scene without venting his wrath on the prisoners—a miracle in itself. The Jewish laborers offered silent thanks to G-d for sparing their lives, and resumed their back-breaking and heart-breaking work. Rabbi Moshe Yechiel went back to work too, but his thoughts remained focused on the tombstone that had refused to crumble under the sledgehammer's blows. "Whose is it?" he wondered. "Whose merit is so great?"

When dusk came, heralding the end of the exhausting workday, he could no longer contain his curiosity. With a silent prayer that he remain undetected, he slithered on his belly among the graves until he reached the mysterious tombstone. Brushing the dust from the words lettered there, he craned his neck to read the name etched into the stone. It said: "Sarah Schenirer."

(Related by HaRav Yechezkel Besser, zt"l, who heard it from Rabbi Moshe Yechiel Skozialitz himself)

Sarah Schenirer's power lingers on into our own time, and it resides in the hands of Jewish women. Our Sages, *zt"l*, have taught us that "it was in the merit of righteous women…that Israel was redeemed from Egypt" (*Sotah* 11b). Also with regard to the future Redemption, we are told, "The generations are not redeemed except through the merit of the generation's righteous women" (*Midrash Zuta Rus*, parashah 4, p. 5 [11]).

What is the secret hidden in our Sages' words? The Jewish woman's mission is crucial to the survival of our nation. Our Sages tell us, "Everything comes from the woman" (*Bereishis Rabbah* 17:7). This is a reality that is easily observable in daily life. "Rabbi Yosi said, 'I have never called my wife, 'my wife,' but rather, 'my home'" (*Shabbos* 118b). The words "wife" and "home" are virtually synonymous. A woman has the power to keep her family's life running smoothly, by focusing inward, on the home. She has the power to fill her home with spirituality. This is the only way to fight back and to erect a formidable barrier against the street's glittering but artificial attractions. A woman who turns her gaze outward and introduces the street's emptiness into her home cannot properly fill her role as a Jewish wife and mother.

We live too close to the seductive but empty "street." Despite our greatest efforts, its influence may creep in through cracks in the walls of our fortresses and towers. There are no stores that sell protective devices to guard our families against outside influences. A woman, however, has it in her power to protect the members of her family, and to immunize them in good time against the destructive influence of outside allurements. At the same time, she must stand guard, doing everything in her ability to prevent the encroachment of these insidious influences.

Gabriel and Michael were medical-school students. Gabriel wanted to become a village doctor, while Michael had ambitions to become a world-renowned physician. When their years in medical school were over, Gabriel was indeed chosen to serve as the doctor of a small village, while Michael went on with his studies. Eventually, he become a famous surgeon. In the course of his career he served in various administrative positions in the medical world, and was finally appointed head of his country's Health Ministry.

One year, a terrible epidemic spread through the country, taking a high toll in lives. His secretary entered Michael's office with a newspaper article, describing how a certain small village had not suffered a single death in the plague.

Michael sat up in his plush executive chair. "Bring me the doctor of that village!" he ordered. "I must find out why no one in his village has died from the plague. What is his secret?"

The next day, the village doctor appeared in Michael's office. One look was all Michael needed to recognize Gabriel, his old friend and fellow student.

"Tell me, Gabriel," Michael said as he shook his friend's hand, "what kind of medicine have you been giving the people of your village when they've fallen ill during this epidemic? Give me the ingredients of the compound at once, so that we may save the citizens of this entire country!"

Gabriel smiled. "You don't understand," he said simply. "The people of my village have not died because they have not become infected with the plague. When I became their doctor, my primary mission was disease prevention. I gave the village folk lectures on proper nutrition and proper physical exercise, and did my best to build up their immune systems. By now, their bodies are strong and protected enough to keep them from contracting the disease."

This is the role of the woman—the homemaker—who is the essence of the home. She must build up her family's "immune system" so that they will not be infected with the "disease" that runs rampant through the world's streets.

"Her husband's heart relies on her" (Mishlei 31:11). The woman in this verse is praised for being someone who can be relied upon. Indeed, one of the outstanding attributes of a "woman of valor" is her ability to recognize the fact that we are influenced by our surroundings, to take the necessary steps to protect herself and her loved ones from destructive influences, and to recruit the assistance of desired influences.

The Mishnah in *Pirkei Avos* describes the greatness of the Tanna, Rav Yehoshua, with the words "Praiseworthy is she who bore him!" (*Avos* 2:11). His wise mother understood the power of the environmental influence. She placed his cradle in the study hall, so that even in earliest infancy his ears would absorb the sounds of Torah study.

When we see the enormous power of positive influence, it is not difficult to acknowledge the potential damage of negative influence.

Women were given the ability to distinguish between positive and negative influences, and to steer their families in the right direction. "The wisdom of women built her home" (Mishlei 14:1). Women build their homes through the use of their wisdom. Every woman is born with this ability, though sometimes she has to learn how to use it.

"How goodly are your tents, O Yaakov, your dwelling places, O Yisrael!" (Bamidbar 24:5). The word "goodly" hints at the woman, as in the saying "He who has found a woman has found something good" (Mishlei 18:22). "Come and see how good a good woman is, as the Scripture has called her a good find.... She is called good" (*Pesikta Zutrasa, Tazria* 33b). A woman has the power to turn her home into a miniature Holy Temple. She is the one with the ability to take her "Yaakov" and turn him into a "Yisrael"—the higher level of a Jew.

In many communities, it is customary for a Jewish bride to circle her groom under the wedding canopy. The circling is meant to symbolize the fact that, with this marriage, the woman will serve as a protective wall for her husband and safeguard him. In order to fulfill this protective role, the woman herself must be protected. The laws of modesty are her primary weapon in achieving this goal. Accordingly, safeguarding her modesty is of paramount importance to her and her family.

The woman was chosen to be her family's protector. This is a responsibility of the highest order. She must safeguard her inner essence—for the sake of her home. What are the tools and means that she has been given in order to achieve this goal?

Chapter 4

Recognizing the Challenge

The first enemy is—compromise.

It is all too easy to adopt an attitude of compromise and feel that we're just fine. After all, we keep the mitzvos and attend good schools. Certainly, all those who are bemoaning the dreadful situation and calling for improvement don't have *us* in mind!

Sometimes, however, someone steps into our midst from the outside, and shows us the reality.

It had been a long journey, but Aliza was happy now. She and her husband were ba'alei teshuvah in the full sense of the word. Both of them had joyfully and enthusiastically embraced the Torah lifestyle that they'd first learned about only a year earlier.

One day, Aliza was leafing through a magazine when

she came upon an ad offering a Shabbos in a luxury hotel. The offer included Torah lectures by well-known speakers, the highest level of kashruth observance and a peaceful atmosphere. Everything seemed just right. Aliza called up and reserved places for her husband and herself.

By the end of Shabbos, however, she did not feel any exaltation of the spirit. "I thought I was finished with all of that," she said, disappointed. "I thought all that glitter belonged to my past. But in that hotel, I kept coming across immodesty over and over again. True, the women were covered up…but many of them looked eye-catching and provocative to me!"

Recognizing the problem is half the solution. Acknowledging that there's room for improvement is the first step in achieving it; after that, it is possible to move on toward an understanding of how we've reached the undesirable situation in which we find ourselves, and how we can truly change it. In order to recognize the challenge facing us, it is crucial that we analyze our attitude toward the all-important mitzvah of modesty.

The Prophet Yirmiyahu asks: "Why did we lose the Holy Temple?"

The *Yalkut Shimoni* (Yirmiyahu, *remez* 281) relates that our Sages attempted to answer this question but were unsuccessful. Then the prophets and the angels tried to answer it, but they too could not. Only G-d Himself is capable of providing the answer to such a question: "Because they have abandoned My Torah…" (Yirmiyahu 9:12).

The midrash offers an explanation by Rav Yehuda, in Rav's name, about the nature of the sin mentioned in this verse. He says, "Because they did not recite a blessing before [studying Torah]." In other words, the destruction of the Holy Temple came about because the people did not recite the blessing over the Torah.

Rabbeinu Yona interprets this to mean that Torah study was not sufficiently important in the people's eyes to make them feel the need to recite a blessing over it.

We see, then, that the Destruction came about because of a flaw in attitude and perspective. Because of a lack of proper appreciation for the Torah.

There is another example of the consequences of not having enough appreciation for G-d's word: the shattering of the Tablets of the Covenant. When Moshe descended from Mount Sinai and saw the people dancing around the Golden Calf, he threw the Tablets down to the ground (*Shemos* 32:19). How could Moshe have done such a thing?

The Tablets were fashioned in such a way that it was possible to read them from either side. Where the letters were etched, there was no stone at all. When the Jews sinned, the letters flew heavenward, leaving the gaps to fill up with stone in their place. This, our Sages teach, made the Tablets so very heavy—too heavy for Moshe to bear. He was forced to cast them to the ground. "Why didn't Moshe drop the Tablets the moment G-d told him that the Jews had fashioned a calf? Because, as the *Yalkut* (*remez* 393) says: 'Because the letters departed, the stone became heavy and fell from Moshe's hands'" (Kli Yakar on *Shemos* 32:16).

If we delve a little more deeply, we can learn a lesson from this incident that applies to every Jew, in every day and age. That is: The Torah becomes a burden only when it is unappreciated.

The Dubno Maggid brings this idea to life with a parable that he devised about the words of the verse: "But you did not call out to me, O Yaakov, for you grew weary of Me, O Yisrael" (*Yeshayahu* 43:22):

> *Reuven, a successful diamond dealer, had a special servant who carried his bags whenever Reuven returned from a business trip. At the end of one trip, the servant carried the suitcases, as usual. What was unusual was the way he was*

puffing and panting as he did so.

"My goodness, how heavy these bags are!" he groaned, in the hope that Reuven would give him a generous tip.

Upon hearing these words, Reuven fainted.

When he revived, his servant hastened to explain himself. "I'm sorry," he said. "I didn't mean to say anything that would upset you that much. I only thought that I deserved an extra-large tip today because the suitcases are so much heavier than they usually are."

Reuven fainted again!

When his master had regained consciousness, the servant kept silent, afraid to say a word lest he cause any more damage. He certainly did not wish to cause his master to faint a third time...

"Do your ears hear what your mouth is saying?" Reuven asked at last, speaking with difficulty. "I am a diamond dealer. Diamonds are a commodity that weighs hardly anything at all. If my bags are heavier than usual this time, it must be that someone has stolen my diamonds—and substituted rocks and stones in their place!"

G-d's commandments are comparable to diamonds, which do not weigh much. If we feel as though we are carrying heavy boulders, something is wrong. It's all a matter of attitude. It is our task to transform our heavy stones into sparkling diamonds. If we do that, then we'll be the first ones to want to improve ourselves, and to seek out the ways to do so.

This principle holds true for the commandments regarding modesty, as well. The deeper our appreciation for this mitzvah grows, the easier it will be for us to keep it. A princess living in a palace does not feel suffocated or depressed by the king's laws. She knows that they're designed to deepen her connection to the royal dynasty! A royal princess must adhere to the king's laws; should she try to free herself of them and escape the rules of royalty, she will become just an ordinary citizen. A genuine princess longs to fulfill the king's injunctions and listens to every word that he utters. In this way, she will grow increasingly close to her father, the king, and merit more of his protection.

Every Jewish woman is a daughter of the King of kings. He has given her these commandments for her own benefit. But sometimes, because she doesn't understand this, she tries to run away—to escape what she perceives as a host of "restrictions and limitations." She turns off the tape recorder so as not to listen to an inspiring lecture and closes the book when she sees what it's about. "Oh, no! Not the subject of modesty again" is her automatic reaction.

She feels as if she's doing G-d a favor if she adheres—more or less—to the laws of modesty. What more is there for her to learn on this subject? She's afraid of hearing things that, to her mind, seem to be limitations and stringencies. She wants to run away from all this, because she feels that following the guidelines is a heavy burden that is too difficult for her. She sees no point in investing great effort in this area.

In actual fact, every restriction is another rung in the ladder "whose feet rest on the ground and whose head touches the heavens." Another rung closer to the King. The woman who takes the trouble of climbing it will reap the fruits of her efforts in both the present and the future. The moment she realizes the advantages and the profit, she will stop wanting to run away and will instead seek out every means of improvement. To achieve this goal, all she has to do is understand what the mitzvah of modesty is really all about, and how much it offers the Jewish woman. That's all it takes.

The Midrash (*Bereishis Rabbah* 44:1) tells us: "The mitzvos were given in order to refine mankind." The Torah's commandments are meant to help us improve and elevate ourselves as human beings. A woman's task is to use these commandments as a tool with which to elevate herself and her family. The Hebrew word *hachein*—"the grace"—is an acronym for a woman's three primary mitzvos: *hadlakos haner*, *challah*, and *niddah* (lighting Shabbos candles, separating *challah*, and observing the laws of *taharat hamishpachah*). Literally, the word *hachein* refers to personal charm. To fulfill these three mitzvos in the best possible way—one that will lead to the aforementioned goal—a woman must be genuine on the inside. The personal charm of a Jewish woman is her modesty. With it, she can attain that longed-for inner self.

HaGaon Rav Yitzchak Zilberstein, *shlita*, describes the following episode:

> *In a certain city, I met a woman who did not appear to be Torah-observant, yet she had brought her daughter to be registered in a religious school. Surprised, I asked her, "Why have you decided to give your daughter this kind of education? From the look of things, it's not the sort of education that you were given."*
>
> *The woman replied, "Two girls came to my house and spoke to me about registering my daughter in a religious school. Those girls were so modest, so unassuming! I was very impressed by their special charm. I thought to myself, 'I wish my daughter could be that way!'*
>
> *"Right then and there, I made up my mind to give her the kind of education that reaps such fruits...."*

The primary mitzvah incumbent upon Jewish women—a mitzvah that the Vilna Gaon compares to the mitzvah of Torah study for men—is that of modesty. We all try to be modest, but we don't always give it the attention it deserves. We must realize that we are facing an enormous challenge. The glittering world around us has taught and is teaching women across the globe to attract attention—deliberately or unwittingly.

Our women too live in the world. And like it or not, they are influenced by the current trends. Sometimes they make the mistake of attracting the wrong kind of attention—not deliberately, perhaps, but unintentionally, simply through not being aware. They are either oblivious of some of the small details and subtleties, or they don't take them seriously enough. The inevitable result is that they end up breaching the protective fence that the Torah has erected around them to shield them from strangers' eyes.

Even women who try to be scrupulous about observing this mitzvah don't always grasp the depth of this matter, because they don't fully understand the significance of a lack of modesty. They just don't understand what it is that makes men look at them.

What our women have to do now is move forward in their awareness of this mitzvah. They must take the concepts of modesty that they've been using until now, and put their hearts and souls into the search for an even deeper knowledge, so that they may flourish in this special mitzvah that is uniquely theirs. They need a change of attitude: an earnest desire to improve. "Modesty is most praiseworthy, and [a woman] should surround herself with it on every side, so that there is no breach anywhere upon her" (Rabbeinu HaMeiri, on *Shabbos* 113b).

The "Modesty Revolution" will strengthen and increase our vitality, both in this world and in the next. Is there any woman who would not want to be part of such a revolution?

Chapter 5

Understanding the Solution

Most people do not like to be told what to do. How much more so, when it's a question as personal as one's dress and outward appearance? It's much easier to shake off criticism with a comment such as, "My style of dress is my own, personal business!"

A person may make the mistake of believing that "freedom" means a complete absence of limits and boundaries. But a person who lives without restrictions becomes in essence a slave to his desires and passions. He is not free at all. In contrast, a person who subjugates himself to G-d's will—who binds himself to the Torah and its laws—is a truly free individual: free of the tyranny of his desires and inclinations and not limited by them. As our Sages teach: "You can have no freer man than the one who engages in the study of Torah" (*Avos* 6:2).

The desire to be beautiful is part of a woman's nature. Any woman, at any age, enjoys a compliment on the way she looks. She must work to control this desire, lest she be swept away to the point where she loses a sense of proportion in this area, and becomes enslaved to her yearning to be beautiful.

The glorification of external beauty is not a Jewish concept; it derives from Greek culture. The Torah regards the body as the clothing of the soul. In the Jewish view, the essence of an individual is what's on the inside, and not his outward appearance. Moreover, the more the body is covered and concealed, the more the soul—which is the true person—will shine forth. Grasping the nature of true beauty, as taught by the Torah, is essential for women, because these concepts are inextricably bound up in their nature. Their happiness depends on their properly understanding them.

Our Sages, *zt"l*, have defined the concept of "beauty" with enormous clarity. "There is nothing more beautiful than modesty" (*Tanchuma*, *Ki Sisa* 31). In other words, modesty *is* beauty because it allows the soul to shine forth, leaving the body in the background. A genuine and lasting satisfaction can come only from the spiritual. The entire physical, material dimension is ephemeral: here today, gone tomorrow. Therefore, a woman must take care not to distort the soul's central role through emphasizing her external appearance.

We can learn this from our matriarch, Leah. Rabbi Meir of Premishlan, *zt"l*, said: "Leah deliberately indulged in copious weeping, from fear that she would fall to Eisav's lot. She hoped [through all this crying] to make her eyes weak and her countenance ugly, so that Eisav would not wish to marry her. Therefore, the Targum translates the words 'Leah's eyes were tender' (Bereishis 29:17) as 'Leah's eyes were fitting or becoming.' The softness in Leah's eyes *was* their beauty, because it had come about through fear of Heaven, lest she fall to a wicked man's lot.

There is no beauty greater than this" (*Ma'ayana shel Torah*, p. 132).

The way to be more beautiful is to be more modest. The laws of modesty, in all their myriad details, are designed not only to protect the woman—by erecting a barrier between her and men who are not her husband—but also to highlight her true beauty. The perception of this special beauty imbues a woman with a sense of value and self-respect, and gives her a marvelous feeling of personal contentment and the authentic satisfaction that belongs to everyone who lives their life according to the Creator's commandments.

Every woman must recognize the special privileges that she enjoys by virtue of the fact that she is a princess. All Jewish women, whatever their background, origin, or age, are daughters of the King. All their souls stood together at the foot of Mount Sinai and heard Him proclaim, "I am Hashem, your G-d" (Shemos 20:2). The words "I am Hashem" constitute the essence of every Jewish woman's soul. As she chooses her wardrobe, as she decides what kind of look to adopt and what sort of image to broadcast, those words are echoing inside her: "I am Hashem."

G-d created us, and He has given us guidelines about how to conduct ourselves. He created us with free will, and He will reward us endlessly for the right choices that we make over the course of our lives. We can choose to protect our souls, or we can allow them to spill out and roll around in the streets. The choice is ours.

The Creator created a world in which men are attracted to women. Without this reality, the world would cease to exist. It is up to the woman to realize that she is an attracting force. In light of this, and as a declaration of her faith in the Creator of the world and the purpose for which He created it, she must conceal her external self. It makes no difference whether or not she understands how or why this attraction principle works. She is obligated to accept the reality of its existence.

Women are capable of being modest. This is no impossible feat. G-d never gives us a challenge that we are incapable of meeting. The clearer our understanding becomes in this area, the easier it will be to do what is required of us.

Modesty is not confined to clothing alone. It expresses itself in the way a woman carries herself, in her body language, in the way she walks, talks, and even in the way she laughs. It is not enough for a woman to be covered up and modestly dressed. Every aspect of her behavior must denote restraint.

Her femininity must be concealed—not because there's something wrong with it, as people who look at modesty superficially sometimes mistakenly believe. On the contrary, a woman was blessed with *binah yeseirah*, an added dimension of wisdom and understanding. When she marries, she knows exactly for whom she's reserving her deep, inner beauty. The modest woman does not share her inner essence with others; she saves it only for her husband. When a man marries a woman, he proclaims, "You are sanctified to me." This signifies that just as the vessels of the Holy Temple are especially designated for that place alone, so too a man's wife is designated only for her husband.

When a woman is confident that she is dressed in accordance with Jewish law, and all of her behavior proclaims her modesty, then she can be tranquil. Uncertainty leads to unhappiness: it is known that "there is no joy like the removal of doubt. As the wise man said, 'No one who has not tasted doubt and its removal has ever tasted joy'" (Responsa of the Ramah, response 5). When a woman reaches a place where she has no more doubt that she is correctly carrying out her Creator's will, she can achieve the true joy that is a necessary and desirable component in every Jew's life. The numerical value of the word *safek*, "doubt." is equal to that of "Amalek," which has the same letters as the word *l'akem*, "to distort." When we distort the law in order to satisfy an agenda of our own, we certainly cannot adhere to it properly. Then doubt will creep into our hearts, leading to a loss of happiness.

The word *besimchah*, "in joy," has the same letters as the word *machshavah*, "thought." We are enjoined to "serve Hashem in joy!" (Tehillim 100:2). Doing the right thing always leads to happiness, which is connected to a feeling of closeness to G-d. The more a person thinks deeply about these things and works hard to attain them, the happier he will feel. When we shake off uncertainty, we become capable of achieving satisfaction. And how do we attain satisfaction? By using our "sixth sense," our extra dimension of intuition, to turn *safek*, "doubt," into *sipuk*—"satisfaction."

We must never downplay the importance of joy. The Jewish people are in exile, "Because you did not serve Hashem, your G-d, amid gladness and goodness of heart" (Devarim 28:47). Rabbi Moshe Feinstein, *zt"l*, once remarked that the often-heard expression "It's hard to be a Jew!" has undermined the foundations of our nation's very existence. A lack of joy can lead only to downfall.

What we need is a thoughtful happiness, achieved through the medium of prior thought. The path to joy is by embracing the mitzvos with elation and pride, in the manner of, "His heart was elevated in the ways of Hashem" (2 Divrei Hayamim 17:6). We do this by feeling immensely lucky to be princesses—those whom the King has personally and individually chosen. The joy that this will generate in us will overwhelm us with endless blessing.

What woman would want to pass up such a golden opportunity?

Chapter 6

Practically Speaking

As we climb the path to self-improvement, knowing the pitfalls along the way is the most practical way to avoid falling into them. The pitfalls are real and tangible, and exposing them can help us properly prepare for them and achieve the hoped-for rectification.

- **The danger of unawareness**. Most women are very busy. They are overwhelmed with things to do—and that's an understatement! They're certainly too busy to constantly check and analyze their wardrobes.

  Leah was going to be late for her appointment. She hurriedly opened her closet, took the first skirt her hand touched, and was on her way. Unfortunately, for the rest of that day she had no idea that she was walking around with her knees showing. Leah had recently gained some weight, a fact that had somewhat altered her shape. The skirt that had been long enough until then was now too short for her.

- **The danger of relying on others**. All too often, we rely on feeble "proofs," such as "The wife of a well-known rabbi wore a dress just like this. That must mean that it's 100% okay!"

  Tzippy was looking for a suit for herself. In a certain store, she found one that she was "positive" she'd seen the wife of their community rabbi wearing. She didn't give the outfit another thought or a second look. "If it's good enough for the rebbetzin, it's certainly good enough for me," she decided, and went straight over to the counter to pay for the suit.

In actuality, the suit was similar to the rebbetzin's, but not identical. And even if it was the exact same outfit, that would not have been enough to verify its "kosher" status. An outfit that looks proper on one person may not look the same on another one. Besides, everyone needs to take responsibility for herself, and not rely on others' judgments.

- **The danger in compromise**. Most women become accustomed to their "look" and are more-or-less satisfied with it. Change is something that rocks the boat, and presents a challenge that one must surmount in order to grow.

  Searching for a weekly class to attend, Dina caught sight of an ad for a class on the topic of modesty. It would be delivered by a well-known speaker, and Dina was interested in hearing what she'd have to say on the subject. But she was afraid of the consequences. She was happy with the way she looked and didn't relish the thought of dealing with the need to change it. She decided that a class on the weekly portion was a safer option.

- **The danger of the word "everyone."** Women are engaged in a constant battle between themselves and "everyone." It's very easy to do what "everyone" is doing. A person must make a focused effort to withstand public opinion and do the right thing—even if "no one" else is doing it.

  Penina stood in the clothing store, holding two items in her hands. One of them, she knew, was perfectly modest. The other was definitely not perfect in that respect—but "everyone" was wearing it. What a difficult choice for such a young woman!

- **The danger of an inauthentic *kiddush Hashem*.** Women have a natural desire to be close to their Creator. Sometimes, however, they make the mistake of thinking that they are sanctifying G-d's Name by presenting a dazzling outward appearance. After all, if people see how gorgeous religious women look, won't they be inspired to embrace a Torah lifestyle, too?

  Her natural beauty, amply assisted by an array of cosmetics, made Yaffa stand out in a crowd. She was convinced that she was a walking kiddush Hashem…until she read an account of a beautiful girl who lived in Talmudic times, and who was praised by our Sages for taking pains to make the exact opposite kind of effort before going out in public, so that men would not be attracted to her.

  Yaffa thought seriously about this story. Maybe she'd been mistaken, she concluded, and she hadn't been sanctifying the Name of G-d after all…

- **The danger of seeking so-called honor.** When a woman regards herself as an object that one can be proud of (as

Queen Vashti was in the eyes of King Achashveirosh), she creates a very low self-image. In a practical sense, her husband's honor is actually harmed when her outward appearance causes other men to find her attractive and not the opposite.

All of her husband's friends and their wives were going to participate in the tenth-anniversary celebration of the yeshivah that Ditza's husband attended. Ditza went to a great deal more trouble than usual to dress in a way that would make her husband proud of her. But she felt very foolish when her husband's rosh yeshivah spoke about the need for Jewish women to work on improving in the area of modesty.

- **The danger in advertisements**. Advertising exerts a powerful influence. If it didn't, people wouldn't waste their money on taking out ads. Women, too, are open to being brainwashed by advertisements that obligate them to "look good." Conversations among women of all ages tends to center around external appearances: wigs, clothing, make-up, and fashion accessories.

Before she was married, Shevi thought it a terrible waste of time to spend all day talking about external appearances. But all that changed the moment she became engaged. She noticed that she too had become caught up in the whirlwind of activity surrounding external appearances, against her natural inclination. "Impossible!" she thought over and over. Nevertheless, she was doing what she never believed she would ever do.

- **The danger in not understanding the possibility of being a stumbling block.** Men and women are two different worlds, and each is incapable of gauging the other by his or her own yardstick. In other words, women don't understand men, nor are they capable of understanding them. Ignoring the inborn differences between men and women is like burying one's head in the sand.

*Enough already! Chaya thought angrily. Once again, the rebbetzin was speaking on the subject of "You shall not place a stumbling block before the blind." Can't men guard their eyes? Why do **I** have to be responsible for **their** failures? And anyway, why are men compared to blind people?*

Chaya decided to speak personally to the rebbetzin about this right after the class. It was only after their talk that, for the first time in her life, she began to understand. She realized that men face their own challenges. They wage a war about which she had no conception.

The danger in fear of failure. Women, like all human beings, are afraid of moving in the direction of a positive change, lest they fail. They're afraid that failing will make them feel foolish, in their own eyes and in the eyes of others.

Chedva left the lecture hall in an exalted frame of mind. How she wanted to muster the strength to move forward! But, at the same time, she was terribly afraid that she would not succeed. Maybe, she thought, if Chaya would be willing to join her, they could take a step forward together. Perhaps that would help.

The Hebrew word *beged*, "an article of clothing," is composed of the same letters as the word *boged*, "traitor." Clothes can betray a woman. *Beged* is comprised of three consecutive letters near the start of the Hebrew alphabet. The word *sheker*, "falsehood," is also composed of three consecutive letters, only in reverse order and near the end of the alphabet. In contrast, the letters of the word *emes*, "truth," are scattered along the whole length of the alphabet, as are those of the word *levush*, "garments."

These days, truth is scattered in bits and pieces, a little here and a little there. As our Sages tell us: "In the generation when the son of David [the Mashiach] will come…truth will be absent…. [Meaning] that [truth] will be fragmented and dispersed among numerous groups [lit. flocks, *adarim*] and from them it will go away" (*Sanhedrin* 97a). There is no concentration of truth in the world today. Falsehood, on the other hand, is both concentrated and powerful.

When the Mashiach comes, he will cause the three letters of the word *emes*—now scattered—to draw close and come together, thus making truth more powerful than falsehood. We find this hinted at in the words of the mishnah, which teaches that Eliyahu the Prophet, who will precede the Mashiach's arrival, will come to "distance those who are near through force and to draw near those who were distanced by force" (*Adiyos* 8:7). It is our aspiration to transform all of our false clothing into garments of truth, and thus help hasten the coming of Eliyahu.

We live in a world where the whole issue of external appearances has taken on a compulsive quality. Our closets are bulging with clothes. People's lives surround the question of what to wear, what to buy, and even what to remove from their overfull closets. This applies, as well, to modest clothing.

The purpose for which clothing was created was to cover human beings and lend them honor (*Bava Kama* 91b)—*not* to cause them to make their outward appearance stand out or to take pride in it. A woman needs to embrace the goal of looking respectable and dignified. Exposing herself only lowers her worth and cheapens her. A Torah scroll is covered with a mantle because its contents are extremely valuable. We could eloquently say that women too should be covered up because they are valuable and important.

Licentiousness is the opposite of modesty. Its Hebrew word *pritzus* implies a breaking-out into a place that is unsuitable. Women are commanded to contain their femininity when they are with other people, because that is not the correct or appropriate place for exposing it. It is not fitting or modest that such a precious, personal, and important part of them should be laid open to all eyes. Such exposure cheapens that which is so very precious.

Our Sages have said: "Intelligence requires a sense of shame, and a sense of shame requires intelligence" (*Orchos Tzaddikim, sha'ar* 3). A person with a sense of shame does not lack intelligence, and an intelligent person does not lack a sense of shame. Modesty, then, is a reflection of intelligence. An intelligent woman who values herself and knows her own worth will do anything to protect it. Is there any Jewish woman who is *not* wise and intelligent?

Chapter 7

Modesty and Marriage

"The Holy One, Blessed is He, gave *binah yeseirah*, an extra dimension of wisdom, to a woman, more than to a man" (*Niddah* 45b). When she marries, a woman's extra wisdom comes into full play. This wisdom is an added and special dimension of intellect, and one of the primary reasons G-d gave it to her is to enable her to carry out her mission as a Jewish wife. This *binah yeseirah* also helps a woman understand the mitzvah of modesty on a deeper level.

Thc only man on earth for whom a woman's charms are reserved is her husband. Therefore, her femininity must be kept in check with regard to all other people. The more a woman internalizes this idea, the more modest she will try to be.

When a girl marries, she faces a big challenge. What is the role of modesty in her life, if she is supposed to look pretty for her husband?

Modesty is a woman's most fundamental trait, and she certainly doesn't throw it out the window after marriage. On the contrary, at this stage in a woman's life her modesty is elevated to a higher level. "A woman must be modest, and take care that no people look at her except for her husband" (*Tanchuma, Vayishlach*).

Married life unites a man and his wife to the level of one body and one soul. The couple, who were originally created as a single unit, join again into a single unit through their marriage. One of the blessings recited under the wedding canopy refers to G-d as the One "Who fashioned man." The marriage bond turns the couple into a single entity, even though the rest of the world sees them as two separate beings. Not only does marriage not nullify a woman's existence—it is the expression of her innermost essence.

Only G-d, Who has given us guidelines for conducting ourselves and our lives, knows what is holy and what is not. Our small minds are incapable of appreciating, measuring, or investigating such deep matters. The unity that is created through the marriage bond is the very essence of holiness. That is why it is hidden from all eyes and extremely private and personal. Exposing it would lower the value of this very precious thing.

In every aspect of modesty, a married woman is at greater risk than one who is single. Now that her femininity is permitted to express itself within the arena of marriage, she must take extra care to protect it when in the company of other people. To aid her in covering and concealing her feminine essence, G-d gave the married woman an additional commandment: to cover her hair. This mitzvah, which we will discuss in depth in the coming chapters, symbolizes the added effort that a woman must make after she marries, to preserve her deep, inner essence for her husband alone.

The more a woman recognizes her own value and holiness, the more aware she becomes that the laws of modesty are meant to act as protection for her, and that they were given to her *because* she is precious and holy. Every morning, women thank G-d "For having made me according to His will" (the morning blessings). And it is G-d's will that they reserve themselves for the other half of their whole, in a way that is private, personal, and exclusive. The moment women understand the holiness of the marriage bond and its spiritual dimension, and the moment they understand the purpose of their essence, they will also comprehend the great need to safeguard it, especially when in the presence of other people.

"A princess whose glory is inward" (Tehillim 45:14). On a practical level, this means that before she steps out of her house, a woman should look in the mirror to make sure that she has succeeded in concealing her femininity. In addition to her obligation to present a respectable appearance, she must make sure that both her external look and her conduct erect a barrier before strangers, to preserve her exclusive status for her husband.

> *"How am I supposed to know what conduct is appropriate for me?" Sima asked her kallah teacher, her pre-marriage instructor.*
>
> *"We're going to learn everything that you need to know. Don't worry about it now," came the confident and reassuring reply. "This is a natural facet of Creation. When you're married, you'll recognize that facet within yourself. But it's important for you to be aware that every woman has to learn to control her special essence. She must learn to conceal it within her when in the company of other people—including, by the way, her father-in-law and brothers-in-law. I'm sure you've learned about Tamar, who merited being the forebear of kings, prophets, and, from her too will come Mashiach. She merited all of that because of her modesty in her father-in-law's house (Megillah 10b).*
>
> *"A married woman has to be constantly aware of her feminine status, which requires extra protection after she marries."*

A woman must erect barriers between herself and other men, in order to avoid any appearance that is attracting or alluring. In a broader sense, she needs to avoid anything that could bring her unique essence to be expressed in a place that is unsuited to it. The moment a woman marries, she begins to be much more in touch with herself. Once she understands the true essence of marriage, she becomes better able than she was in the past to understand the need to protect her own inner essence when in the company of others.

Practically speaking, the more she learns about the marriage bond, the more she comprehends her obligation to appear in public as a person and not as a woman. Her awareness has broadened and her wisdom increased.

Men have been commanded to guard their eyes: "That you may not... explore after your heart and after your eyes" (Bamidbar 15:39). Certainly, women are not interested in being a stumbling-block to make men trip and fall. After all, they've been commanded: "You shall not place a stumbling block before the blind" (Vayikra 19:14). Moreover, expressing one's femininity in the wrong place causes inestimable damage to the woman herself. It causes her to lose a part of her deep and delicate inner essence, leaving that much less for her husband.

What leads to expressing femininity in inappropriate places is a simple lack of understanding. The more she grasps the nature of the marriage bond, the more she will be able to better protect her inner essence—to reserve it for her husband alone and no other man on earth.

Decades of living amid ever-increasing exposure have addled our senses. We feel that we dress much more modestly than "them," so we must be just fine. However, our perceptions of what is "just fine" and what isn't have deteriorated greatly. It's a vicious cycle: our slide down the slippery slope leads the outside world to deteriorate even more; and their downfall encourages us to fall further. On the other hand, were we to improve our levels of modesty, the rest of the world would benefit as well.

This is the route by which G-d wishes to influence the world. When we look at ourselves, we must do so by the light of the most profound, innermost perception and dimension. The spiritual world is the engine that powers the physical one. Every action, thought, and word has an impact on all of existence. G-d chose the Jewish nation to be those who would activate the whole of creation. Even the smallest deeds can have far-reaching consequences for everything that occurs in the world. Members of the Jewish nation exert a powerful influence on one another, even if they have no physical contact at all. As Rav Yisrael of Salant said, "If they gossip in the Kovno *beis midrash* [house of study], they'll be desecrating the Sabbath in Paris" (*Tenuas Hamussar*, part 1, p. 284, para. 10). In the same way, a Jewish woman in New York who switches to a more modest outfit can influence the level of Sabbath observance of a Jewish woman living in Tel Aviv.

Rebbetzin Bas Sheva Kanievsky, *a"h*, told the following story:

> *A group of girls from one of the cities in northern Israel came to see me, and we had a lengthy discussion about the importance of the mitzvah of modesty. They heard, and they acted. On their return to their city, the girls jointly decided to go through their wardrobes, fixing what could be fixed and getting rid of whatever did not conform to Jewish law. Swept up in the joy of doing a mitzvah, they worked together to keep their commitment.*
>
> *At exactly the same time, something happened in that city that could not be called anything but an open miracle. A powerful explosive device, in the hands of terrorists, blew up without harming a single person! When I heard about it, I was extremely moved. It was as clear as the sun that the act*

of self-sacrifice practiced by that group of girls was what had saved thousands of lives. As our Sages tell us: "All Jews are guarantors for one another" (Shavuos 39a).

Immodesty has another consequence. It causes G-d, Who is perfect and Who wants His Creation to achieve perfection, enormous distress. This can lead Him, Heaven forbid, to turn away from us, as it says: "So that He will not see a shameful thing among you and turn away from behind you" (Devarim 23:15). A lack of modesty constitutes a deviation from the perfection that is G-d's goal for His world. This is a betrayal of G-d Himself. The resultant damage affects not only the woman in question, or the man who is attracted to her, but the whole Jewish people and even the entirety of Creation.

Man is G-d's handiwork, and his actions dictate the course of the world. Every action, thought, and deed has its consequences, both positive and negative. G-d, in His compassion, wants us to progress and succeed. He wants our actions to produce positive consequences. When we repent, we demonstrate to Him that we are trying hard to correct our behavior—and then the results of our actions can be positive, despite our slipping. All G-d wants from us is a commitment to improve in the future (based on *Nefesh HaChayim*, *sha'ar* 1).

Yocheved anxiously checked her watch. It was a wintry day, and she'd woken up late. Her bus was due to leave in just fifteen minutes. She threw open her closet door and hastily pulled out an outfit.

She had not yet grown accustomed to the change in her size since her pregnancy. As she was putting on the outfit, she was aware that it was a little small, but she managed to squeeze into it somehow. She did not realize at all that the skirt had become both too short and too tight—not to mention the blouse, which now clung to her in a glaring fashion. Hurrying to the mirror, she threw on some makeup, not noticing how thick and garish the lines were. Then she put on her pretty wig and sprayed herself liberally with her favorite perfume, to make herself feel good after the morning's hectic race to beat the clock.

As she slung her pocketbook over her shoulder, she didn't notice the way the strap pulled the neckline of her blouse much lower than was appropriate. She then ran all the way to the bus stop, her wig bouncing in the wind. Yocheved was a working woman and her home depended on her income. It would not do to be late to work.

A few minutes later, she was seated on the bus, murmuring the words of the morning prayers with concentration. Yocheved had no intention in the world of causing the men on the bus to look at her with such attention. She honestly had no idea that her appearance was so attracting.

Most religious women who dress inappropriately simply have no idea that their appearance attracts men's stares. Thank Heaven, they have not been educated in schools that promoted immodesty. This is the reason it is so imperative to study the subject of modesty. The moment we demonstrate a true desire to improve, G-d showers us with kindness and compassion. He has made it possible for his sons and daughters to cleanse themselves of their sins through the medium of sincere repentance—at any time and at any age.

Ruchama was a sociable and highly intelligent religious woman who faithfully observed the laws of taharat hamishpachah, Shabbat, and kashruth. But the first time she heard about the commandment of modesty was at the age of seventy-seven, in a lecture she attended. Enchanted by what she heard, she looked more deeply into the subject. As a result, she had her immodest clothing altered—and what could not be altered, she simply threw away. Despite comments and raised eyebrows from family and friends, she refused to budge from her decision.

"I always thought that dress was just a question of style," she said. "I never knew that it was connected to Jewish law. I can't describe how good it makes me feel to actually carry out what I've learned. It's never too late!"

Changing one's wardrobe and one's appearance calls for real dedication and self-sacrifice. It's not easy to ignore the comments of friends and family members. It takes a lot of courage to change—but there's no satisfaction like that of a true servant of G-d who does so, instead of continuing to follow the fleeting whims of fashion and other people's opinions. There are no words to describe the feeling of exaltation. This is true freedom and spiritual elevation. This is relating to a person's true, inner essence, the genuine "I," instead of the outward part that people make the mistake of thinking is their true self.

It's important for women to understand that G-d created men and women as two completely different entities. They are different physically and spiritually, inside and out. The differences are many, and men and women must be aware that these differences exist, even if they do not know exactly what they are. A woman cannot even begin to comprehend the challenge that a man faces in trying to guard his eyes as the Torah commands him.

Modesty means hiding everything that's supposed to be hidden. It is bound up in the sense of sight. This sense influences our thoughts, which also make up a hidden part of our beings. Therefore, vision directly impacts the soul. Seeing is believing. Of all the senses, the sense of sight is the most vital. What we see becomes clearly etched in our brains, and acquires a stronger place in our memory and outlook than what we perceive with any of the other senses. As King Shlomo, in his wisdom, said: "Better is what the eyes see than what is imagined" (Koheles 6:9).

Everything a person sees stays with him, whether he wants it to or not. And the influence of what men see is completely different from the influence of the very same sight for women. Women need to be aware of the fact that they don't understand these differences, and therefore they must simply accept G-d's command to make every effort to conduct themselves in a way that will make it easier for men not to be attracted to them.

Even if we don't understand the profound significance of modesty, we can regard it as an opportunity to perform a kindness for a large segment of the Jewish population: the men. Women can help them guard their eyes through the simple expedient of being careful about their appearance and making sure that it is restrained and reserved.

Naturally, a woman wants to look respectable both in her own eyes and in her husband's, and she can do this while making sure that her clothing and her behavior are in accordance with the laws of modesty (chapter 14). The goal of these laws is to ensure that a woman's intellect controls her emotions, and her inner self dominates her outer one. A woman who is scrupulous about observing the laws of modesty will in the future be rewarded in ways and areas too numerous for her to imagine.

"Rabbi Pinchas HaCohen bar Chamah said: When a woman is modest in her home, just as the altar atones, so she too atones for her home—as it says, (Tehillim 128:3): 'Your wife will be like a fruitful vine in the inner chambers of your home'" (*Tanchuma Vayishlach* 6).

To atone for our homes—this is a blessing that includes all other blessings! In a house where sin is atoned for, there is nothing to block Divine blessing from pouring in! What greater merit could a woman possibly seek?

Chapter 8

Hair and Imagination

It was the year 5611 (1851). Rabbi Shimshon Raphael Hirsch, *zt"l*, came to Frankfurt to revive the Jewish community there, which over the passage of time had become a spiritual wasteland. The Reform Movement was active in the city, threatening to wipe out whatever Jewish practice still remained in the community. Only eleven families were still Sabbath-observant, only one youth still put on tefillin, the *mikveh* was closed, there was no kosher slaughtering of animals, and anyone caught ritually circumcising his son was excommunicated.

Rabbi Hirsch was determined to restore the city's spiritual legacy. On his first Shabbos there, he called a meeting. The attendees were not the city's wealthiest people, nor the most influential. The meeting was for the community's women. Rabbi Hirsch impressed upon the women that the community's revival depended on them, because women are the heart and the foundation of the home. Seeing that not a single one of the women covered her hair, he announced that this was the area he wished to address first.

Covering their hair would not be easy, he told them, because foreign winds were blowing and roaring through the city. However, he promised that the first woman who found the courage to undertake this mitzvah would merit having a son who would become a teacher of his generation.

One young woman rose to the challenge and accepted upon herself the mitzvah of covering her hair. Her name was Charlotte Rosenheim, and she was the wife of community member Eliyahu Rosenheim. She served as a role model for the other women, who slowly began to follow her example. In the year 5631 (1871), Charlotte gave birth to a son, whom they named Yaakov.

Many years later, in 5689 (1929), the Agudath Israel held its second Knessiah Gedolah convention in Vienna. Thousands of rabbinical figures flocked to this convention to help strengthen the Torah world. On the seventh day of the historic gathering, Rabbi Meir Shapira of Lublin, *zt"l*, took the floor. He announced that the generation's Torah leaders had decided to honor a certain individual, who was not only great in Torah but tireless in fighting G-d's battles. The man's name was Rabbi Yaakov Rosenheim, of Frankfurt. The assembly went on to bestow on him the honored title of "*Moreinu*"—"our teacher." From that day on, he would be called "*Moreinu* Rabbi Yaakov Rosenheim." This title of honor was signed by the generation's Torah luminaries, including the Chofetz Chaim, Rav Chaim Ozer Grodzinski, and the Gerrer Rebbe.

This was how Rabbi Yaakov Rosenheim acquired that title of honor when he was fifty-eight years old, bringing to fruition Rabbi Shimshon Raphael Hirsch's promise to his mother: that, in the merit of her dedication and self-sacrifice in fulfilling the mitzvah of covering her hair, she would have a son who would become a great leader and teacher among the Jewish nation.

This episode underlines the importance of the mitzvah of hair-covering for the Jewish woman. Unfortunately, this is one of the mitzvos of the Torah that has been less observed in recent generations. There are those who erroneously assume that it is nothing more than a stringency. Others mistakenly believe that it is only a custom. Even among those who know that it is an obligatory commandment, there are women who cover their hair only partially, or with coverings that do not comply with Jewish Law. They do not understand the value of this mitzvah, or its significance.

It is crucial, therefore, to remove the veil from before this important mitzvah and reveal its essence and insights. The more women come to appreciate this mitzvah and to comprehend the concepts that lie behind it, the clearer it will be to them just how far the obligation for a married woman to cover her hair extends, and what constitutes a suitable head covering.

We are obligated to serve Hashem as servants who must carry out our King's will even if we don't understand it. The reasons for the commandments are very profound—far beyond our comprehension—but our Sages have given us a small taste of these reasons, to spur our enthusiasm for observing them.

The Gemara tells of a woman named Kimchis, who lived during the Second Temple era. Kimchis had seven sons, every one of whom merited serving as the *kohein gadol*, the high priest in the Temple—the highest position that a *kohein*, a member of the priestly caste, could hold. Such a thing had never happened before: one woman to have the merit of seeing all seven of her sons serve in such an exalted capacity! When the Sages asked Kimchis what she had done to deserve this merit, she offered an interesting answer: "In all my days, the beams of my house did not see the braids of my hair" (*Yoma* 47a). "When she was able to cover them" (*Tosafos HaRosh*).

Rashi explains this according to the Talmud Yerushalmi (*Yoma* 1:1), basing his explanation on the verse "But the King's daughter is all glorious within, more than in the golden borders of her raiment" (Tehillim 45:14). When a Jewish woman recognizes that her honor is inward and covered, she can merit a great reward—like Kimchis, whose seven sons wore the special golden garments of the *kohein gadol.*

According the Talmud Bavli, however, our Sages did not satisfy themselves with this answer. They continued to ask: "But many women cover their hair. Why don't they merit what you have merited?" The Gemara does not offer an answer to this question, but in light of the Talmud Yerushalmi above, one may perhaps say that the reason for Kimchis's great merit is much more profound. She was not merely scrupulous in her observance of this mitzvah—she also understood its deeper significance. When a woman covers her hair, she causes herself and the entire world to recognize that she is precious and valuable—not because of her outward appearance, but because of her inner content.

Women deserve respect and appreciation for their wisdom, their intelligence, their souls, their sensitivity, and their perception. And it is here, precisely, that the challenge lies. Because women are graced with an attractive external appearance, they are susceptible to being drawn away from their true identity, which is inward and hidden. In life generally, truth is much more often concealed than revealed. G-d is more real than anything we can see or feel with our senses; that is an incontrovertible truth. And yet, this truth is hidden from the eyes of a great many people in the world.

A woman who realizes that her soul, which is a portion of the Divine, is far more real and beautiful than her external appearance, will merit raising children who possess a deep understanding of the inner essence of things. They will recognize the primacy of spirituality and will be in touch with their own inner selves. The most important thing in their lives will be to draw closer to G-d. "A woman who behaves modestly, even if she is an Israelite, is worthy of a *kohein* and will bear *kohanim gedolim*, high priests" (*Bamidbar Rabbah* 1:3).

Many women cover their hair, but few cover it with the awareness that Kimchis had. Kimchis understood the importance of this mitzvah. And that's why she merited what she did.

Rabbi Shemarya Yosef and Rebbetzin Rochel Leah Karelitz, zt"l, lived in Lithuania. They were blessed with nine children. Their sons grew up to be tzaddikim and great Torah scholars, and their daughters were all women of quality. One of their sons became the Chazon Ish, zt"l. One of their sons-in-law was the Steipler Gaon, zt"l.

The Chofetz Chaim once asked Rabbi Meir Karelitz, one of the family's illustrious sons, why his parents had merited such great children.

"Many people used to ask my mother that question," Rabbi Meir replied. "She'd say that she had the custom of every Friday, paying two women to hold a large towel over her when she washed her hair, so that the beams and walls of her house never saw the hair on her head. 'It was well worth the money,' she always said."

What does it mean, not having the beams and walls of her house see her hair?

The foundation upon which a Jewish home is built is different from that of any other home. It is the custom of the world to build houses on very sturdy foundations, buried deep in the ground. The Jewish home, in contrast, is not built from the bottom up—but rather, so to speak, from the top down. The Jewish home derives its essence from the beams of the roof: in other words, from Heaven. Spirituality is what builds the Jewish home and infuses the home with material blessings and success. It all starts at the top, the place we tap into and from which we draw down. In this way, we allow spirituality to infuse our lives—including the material aspects of those lives.

"Through slothfulness the ceiling sags, and through idleness of the hands the house leaks" (Koheles 10:18). The Midrash explains that this verse refers to the Jewish woman. If she does not cover herself properly, the beams of her house will warp and the roof will leak. Scrupulousness in observing the laws of modesty, and especially that of covering the head, is a symbol and a sign that the woman has spread a worthy and good roof over her home. If she exhibits laziness in this area, her ceiling will sag. With diligence, willingness, and effort, she can transform her home into a palace and a miniature Holy Temple.

What is it about hair that lends such significance and far-reaching ramifications to covering it? What *is* hair?

The book of Iyov delves into the question of Divine Providence, and the idea that G-d observes and examines every detail of our world with great precision. Iyov asks the age-old question: Why does there exist in the world the reality of, "A righteous person suffers, while a wicked one prospers"? This seems unjust.

Iyov was a righteous man, a tzaddik, who suffered terrible afflictions. He felt as if G-d had descended on him in a furious storm. It seemed to him as if the world was dominated, Heaven forbid, by wild forces of nature; that everything was confused, as though a tornado had turned the whole world upside-down.

G-d answered this precise aspect of Iyov's question: "G-d then responded to Iyov from out of the storm" (Iyov 38:1). G-d's answer to Iyov's complaint is detailed in the Gemara: "[G-d] said to [Iyov], 'I created many hairs on a person, and for each and every hair I created its own follicle, so that two hairs do not grow from one follicle" (*Bava Basra* 16a).

G-d is telling Iyov: "You are accusing me of descending on you, so to speak, in a storm, a *sa'arah*, and claim that everything in this world is lawless and accidental. I will prove to you that the world is conducted through the most precise Divine Providence. The proof of this is the hair, the *sa'arah*, on your head. (The letters of the Hebrew word *sa'arah* when spelled with the letter *samech* means a storm and when spelled with the letter *sin* means a hair).

"You think that I have confused you with an *oyev*, an enemy [the letters of the Hebrew word 'Iyov' are the same as those in the word *oyev*, 'enemy']. It is not so. I never make a mistake. Contemplate the hair on your head and see how precisely I conduct the world. The head has thousands of hairs, and each hair has its own follicle that brings it nourishment. That is how I created the world, and that is how I conduct it: with the utmost precision of a *chut hasa'arah*, a strand of hair."

The Maharsha expands on this, explaining why hair was the specific example chosen to illustrate G-d's Providence in the world. He stresses that the hair that the verse talks about is specifically the hair that is found on the head. Hair is the least important part of the body. The brain, on the other hand, is the most important part of the body. A person can easily live without hair on his head; its sole purpose is cosmetic. Another characteristic of hair is that it grows all the time. G-d placed hair, the least important part of the body, on top of the brain, the most important part. Hair is made of the body's dead cells, while the brain is the essence of the person.

The hair, of least significance, covers the most vital and significant organ—the brain. Hair symbolizes the trivial details in life, the physical and the nonsensical, while the brain represents intellect and soul—the spiritual side of life. Through the hair on the head that never stops growing, G-d is sending us a message: the brain, which is the essence of the person, pushes hair away from it and rejects it. Hair, the antithesis of what the human being stands for and wishes to achieve, is constantly pushed out and away.

Every part of the body is there to teach us something. The proximity of hair and brain too carries a spiritual message for us. Whereas the rest of the body's parts have a more-or-less fixed shape, hair has various characteristics that differ from person to person. It does not have a single, uniform appearance. Hair can be curly or straight; it appears in different colors and shades; and it can be styled in a variety of ways. Just as a person can choose to arrange his unimportant hair in any way he likes, so too he can decide how to use the non-essential things in his life.

A woman who conducts herself the way Kimchis did will merit both *kemach* (literally, flour; in other words, material prosperity) and holiness. In the merit of a woman who covers her hair, the home will be blessed with both spiritual and material plenty.

In the Temple era, there was a certain kohein who earned his living by inspecting lesions on a person's skin, to determine whether the person was afflicted with a condition known in the Torah as tzara'as. Because he was not earning enough to support his family, the kohein decided to leave Eretz Yisrael and go abroad in an effort to increase his income.

Because he knew that people were used to coming to him with their lesions, he decided to teach his wife the art of distinguishing between the various types of lesions so that she'd be able to answer their questions in his absence. One of the primary symptoms of tzara'as is a white hair on white skin, so the kohein began teaching his wife the laws pertaining to hair.

"Every hair has its own 'spring' to draw from," he told his wife. 'With Divine Providence, each and every hair comes equipped with its own, unique, individual source of nourishment."

"My dear husband," the wife told the kohein, "let your ears hear what your mouth is telling you. If G-d created each hair along with its own source of sustenance—how much more so did He create you with a source of sustenance! Is the Creator incapable of sustaining you in Eretz Yisrael? Don't you see that He is merely testing your faith and your trust in Him?"

"My wife is right," the kohein decided—and remained in Eretz Yisrael.

(Pesikta Zutrasa, Parashas Metzora)

The *kohein*'s wife understood the message concealed in hair. Each individual hair reflects the intelligence, Divine Providence, and caring that G-d exhibits toward every detail of His Creation—with awesome precision. "Every blade of grass below has [an angel] appointed to it from Above, to protect it and to tell it, 'Grow...' " (*Zohar, behashmatos* to *Bereishis, siman* A). A woman who grasps this idea merits bringing the blessing of material plenty into her home.

When G-d created the first man, the greatest gift He gave him was Chava, his wife. Chava was created in such a way that all of her limbs reflected her purpose in life.

"Then Hashem G-d fashioned the rib that He had taken from the man into a woman, and He brought her to the man" (Bereishis 2:22). One can interpret this verse as telling us that G-d created—fashioned—Chava as a complete entity, a finished creation. In finishing off this creation, He formed her hair with a fixed style: a braid (*Eruvin* 18a). Chava's hair did not spread out, but was like a building set on the ground. Her hair was not free and wild, so she had no need to arrange it. Why was her hair the final thing that G-d made in fashioning Chava?

G-d created Chava to serve as Adam's *ezer k'negdo* –"a helpmeet against him." The Netziv, *zt"l*, comments that the biggest help a woman can give her husband is sometimes by opposing him (*Harchev Davar* on Bereishis 2:18). In other words, when necessary, she can restrain him when he loses control. If he becomes angry, she can calm him. If he eats too much, she can help him set limits. If he is too haughty and conceited, she can help tame his feelings of arrogance. A woman takes care of her husband by protecting him from walking in harmful paths. As the Talmud says, "A woman is her husband's helpmeet, the one who illuminates his eyes and stands him on his feet" (*Yevamos* 63a).

Wild hair is symbolic of a lack of control. Braided hair, in contrast, symbolizes restraint and self-control. The fashioning of Chava's hair in the form of a braid constituted a declaration that a woman's mission in life is to make sure that all matters remain under control. Braided hair, then, is emblematic of her job in the home: to serve as the brakes when necessary.

On a deeper level, the brain is divided into two parts: the power of reason, which is the intellectual aspect, and the power of the imagination, which is the aspect that is illogical and unrestrained. The serpent that lured Chava into sin represents the power of the imagination: the power to distort reality and make it appear different than it is (*Seforno* on Bereishis). This irrational way of thinking is our bitterest and most difficult enemy. Irrational thought has the power to change our grasp of the truth and cause us to deviate from it. Our inborn logic allows us to cleave to the truth; the irrational aspect of our minds stands in logic's way.

In our every waking moment, these two opposing parts of our brain are engaged in ceaseless warfare. The Chazon Ish, *zt"l*, explains this idea as follows:

The power of the imagination, being shallow and non-analytical, causes a distortion of our normal thought processes. The imagination views everything in a superficial dimension, and prevents anyone who looks at truth through its lens from examining things deeply (*Emunah U'Bitachon* 1). The imagination possesses special, powerful abilities that allow it to ambush a person's thinking, persuading him that the imaginary premises it has laid out for him are actual facts. It succeeds in attaining total control over a person's thoughts, until the intellect begins behaving like a prisoner. He refuses to inspect the details of the picture that the imagination has painted.

The rational component of the mind is the sworn enemy of the irrational component. The rational part warns the individual not to listen to the irrational part, because it is not responsible. However, despite these repeated warnings, again and again the irrational component often succeeds in defeating the person and conquering the intellect, because it's always ready to jump to conclusions and make hasty, whirlwind decisions. Logic, on the other hand, is far slower and more methodical. It weighs every word, every action, and every step. The imagination traps the intellect in a *sa'arah*, a storm, before the intellect has a chance to figure out its next step with its characteristic precision, *k'chut hasa'arah*, as fine as a strand of hair.

This is life's greatest test. Do we view life as a storm, a tornado that turns the world upside-down without rhyme or reason—or, like a strand of hair, a creation uncanny in its precision?

Torah study is the best counterforce to the imagination, because "imagination" is only another word for the *yetzer hara* or "evil inclination." Its mission is to confuse us, to suck us into the storm's vortex. Despite the voice of reason, we are all too likely to be drawn into the whirlpool—unless we recruit Torah to our aid. As the Gemara says: "G-d told Yisrael: My children, I have created the evil inclination, and I have created the Torah as its antidote. If you engage in Torah [study], you will not fall into his hands" (*Kiddushin* 30b).

If we live in the world of Torah and reason, everything is as precise and organized as a strand of hair. The more we learn the Torah and scrupulously observe its laws, *k'chut hasa'arah*, the more we will absorb the fact that G-d conducts His world down to the tiniest and most subtle details. Every cell, every electron, every miniscule thing, even if we can't see them, are testament to Divine Providence in this world.

If we study the individual hairs on a person's head, we will observe tremendous individual providence, logic, and careful planning. On the other hand, if we look at all of the hair as a single unit, we will see a complete *lack* of order. Hair seems to spring forth impetuously, out of control, like a storm.

Women have the strength to control their hair, which represents the mind's irrational aspect. Their head-covering symbolizes this power. What woman would not want to be proud of this, and cover her hair?

Chapter 9

Royal Crown

Before G-d gave Chava to Adam, the first man, He bestowed a gift upon her: "*binah yeseirah*," a special intuition or power of understanding. Our Sages derive this from the verse: "*Vayiven Hashem Elokim es hatzelah*—Then Hashem G-d fashioned the rib [that he had taken from the man into a woman]" (Bereishis 2:22). The word *vayiven*, "fashioned," comes from the same root as the word *binah*, "wisdom" (*Niddah* 45b).

Every woman stands under her wedding canopy with this special intuition in her suitcase, so to speak. She is commanded to cover her hair from her wedding day forward. Through this, she demonstrates her appreciation for the gift she's been given, *binah yeseirah*, which resides in the brain, underneath her hair. With the aid of this wisdom, she will build her home.

When bride and groom stand beneath the *chuppah*, the wedding canopy, it is as if they are standing beneath the wings of the *Shechinah*, the Divine Presence. When she covers her hair, the bride is figuratively carrying the *chuppah* around with her wherever she goes. Her head-covering is like a canopy that bestows upon her unending blessing. In wearing it, she celebrates her marriage all the days of her life. Thanks to her head-covering, her marriage enjoys a constant sense of freshness and vitality, and the couple spend their entire lives together feeling as if they are newlyweds.

The word *vayiven*, then, has two connotations that do not contradict one another. It refers to G-d's fashioning of Chava's body and hair, as well as to the special wisdom He implanted in her and in all women after her. Chava's mission was to take care not to let herself be swept away by her imagination—by the irrational.

But the story ended in tragedy. The serpent, which caused the tragedy, symbolizes the imagination. Just as a distorted mirror presents the eye with an optical illusion and makes people appear very different than they do in reality, so too was the serpent able to distort the appearance of reality. He was irrational, and he was able to distort Chava's grasp of reality in sufficient measure to make her pay attention to the falsehoods he was telling her.

Chava was the luckiest woman on earth. She lived in the Garden of Eden and was permitted to eat from any tree in the Garden—except for one, the *Eitz HaDa'as*, the Tree of Knowledge. In his sly, underhanded way, the serpent managed to worm his way into Chava's imagination and convince her that she had nothing in her life. "You have a fine life," he hissed sweetly into her ear, "but you have never tasted of the Tree of Knowledge. Because of that, everything you have is worthless. You have never really enjoyed life."

So strong and persuasive was the power of the imagination that Chava felt as if her life was flat and meaningless. If she could not taste of the Tree of Knowledge, she was surely living in *Gehinnom*, Hell.

After she failed this test, Chava was afflicted with ten disadvantages (*Eruvin* 100b). Chava had not made use of the greatest gift she possessed: her *binah yeseirah*. She had not utilized her intellect. She had not put on the brakes and exercised self-control. Instead, she had reached out her hand without restraint to take the one thing that had been forbidden her. One of the consequences of her action was that from then on, her hair would no longer have a fixed style. As our Sages taught: "What is the meaning of *vayiven* ['He fashioned']?... To teach that G-d braided Chava's hair and brought her to Adam" (*Eruvin* 18a). After the sin, "Her hair grew wild, like the hair of a demon" (*Eruvin* 100b). This was the exact opposite of the way she'd been created—the way that things were meant to be.

Chava's life after the sin was completely different from her life before the sin. She now had to go about with her head covered, like a woman in mourning. She was embarrassed to walk around with her hair uncovered (*Eruvin* 100b). Her head-covering was a sign that she needed to control the irrational. From that point on, G-d would no longer hold her hair together in a fixed and orderly braid. Now Chava had to make the effort herself and see to it that her hair was covered. This was a significant shift in terms of women's nature.

Sounds and sights have the capacity to rapidly change shape once they've entered the human mind, taking on strength and power far surpassing their real-life dimensions. When it's dark outside and a person sees a shadow, he is liable to jump to the conclusion that it's a terrifying monster.

A salient characteristic of demons is an abundance of hair (*Midrash Rabbah*, Bamidbar 12:2). This symbolizes lack of control, the absence of reason, and a wild imagination. In the Torah (Vayikra 17:7), these demons are called hairy ones, *se'irim*, from the root *se'ar*, which means "hair." Eisav, who stands for the powers of impurity, is called Se'ir. Today, we live in the exile known as "Edom"—which is Se'ir—it is incumbent upon us to remember always that Se'ir is the opposite of Torah.

The Hebrew word for a demon is *sheid*. This word is composed of the letters *shin* and *daled*. In contrast, one of G-d's Names is composed of the letters *shin*, *daled*, and *yud*. The extra letter, *yud*, is a rectification of the *sheid*. When we walk out of a room, we kiss the mezuzah, whose outside bears G-d's Name: *shin*, *daled*, and *yud*. This name is an acronym for the words "*Shomer Delatos Yisrael*"—Guardian of the doors of Yisrael. G-d is the One who stands guard, so to speak, over the doors of the Children of Israel.

A mezuzah must be rolled up and not exposed. For demons and the forces of impurity, the world is a wide-open place—a lawless, anarchic free-for-all. The forces of impurity have no dominion over closed, sealed things (*Chullin* 105b). Their dominion extends only to things that are open. Protection against them is the *shin*, *daled*, and *yud* written on the rolled-up mezuzah.

Another message sent to us in the name *shin*, *daled*, and *yud* is that "when G-d created the world, it expanded and grew...until He told the world, '*Dai*—Enough!'" (*Chagigah* 12a). G-d has instructed us to control and restrain ourselves. When He created the world, He sent out in all directions the forces of restraint, halting, and control. These powers were built into the very fabric of Creation, as the purpose of the world's creation was for humankind—men and women alike—to act while exerting self-control.

The mezuzah on our doorpost reminds us that we must live within the borders set by *shin*, *daled*, and *yud*—in a world of self-control. On the one hand, the world has an intrinsic capacity for expansion: the power to go out and explore. On the other hand, we must be aware that unfettered exploration carries an inherent danger that individuals will engage in improper conduct (*Chagigah* 12).

The home is a protected place. The moment we set foot outside its four walls, we expose ourselves to the danger of losing our self-control. Therefore, as we walk out the door we kiss the mezuzah, as if to say, "Master of the Universe, send Your angels to watch over me, lest I stray into a place that is not fitting for me."

After the sin, Chava's freedom of choice expanded from a limited choice concerning a single act—eating from the Tree of Knowledge—to the obligation to choose the correct action with every step taken. When she was created, her hair was fixed and orderly. After the sin, in which she did not make proper use of her *binah yeseirah*, this natural gift was taken away from her. But the only thing she lost was her fixed hairstyle—an external defense against breaching borders. She was still left with her innate wisdom, which enables her to identify the borders on her own so that she can be careful not to cross them. Now, after the sin, she was required to cover her hair. She had to become holy and restrained, to bring to fruition the powers of the *shin-daled-yud* that are represented by the mezuzah.

> *Many people used to bring money to Rabbi Meir of Premishlan, for distribution to charity. Despite the fact that he was destitute, he never took any of these funds for himself or his own family.*
>
> *One day, a childless man came to him and begged for a blessing that he would have a child. Nine months later, the man was embracing a son. As a token of his gratitude, he*

sent Rabbi Meir 300 rubles—an enormous sum in those days. As usual, Rabbi Meir planned to distribute the money to the poor.

"How can I keep the money for myself?" he thought. "That man sent it to me because he believed that my blessing brought about his salvation. In truth, however, he is mistaken. It was his own prayers that brought about his salvation."

When his close friends pressured him to keep the money for his family, and even cited the opinion of a Torah authority whom they'd consulted on the matter, which stated categorically that the money was his to use, Rabbi Meir replied that because the matter was unclear, he had to consult with his wife. He explained that when they had married, they had agreed between themselves only to derive benefit from things that had no halachic doubts pertaining to them. "If a doubt has been raised concerning this money," he said, "it does not belong to us."

Rabbi Meir's wife, when consulted, concurred completely with her husband. By mutual consent, they did in fact distribute the money to the poor.

When doubts arise, the imagination may step in and cause things to appear different than they are in actuality. Here is where the woman's *binah yeseirah* enters the picture. Rabbi Meir of Premishlan, a righteous and G-d-fearing man, understood that, when uncertain how to act, he must consult with his wife. He did not want to rely on his own wisdom alone; he chose to be assisted with his wife's extra dimension of wisdom. A woman has a delicate sensibility and a deep understanding, and she must use these in the correct manner. To the degree that she makes proper use of her *binah yeseirah*, she will be a queen in her palace.

A woman has to believe in herself and in the *binah yeseirah* with which she has been graced. She is obligated to remain in control, so that her husband and children too may be in control. A man who goes out into the world, the Midrash tells us, needs a wife to protect him. Women who cover their hair are, in effect, declaring that they are in control of their intellect and do not permit the power of the imagination to influence them. In this way, they are able to fulfill their tasks and protect their husbands in the most effective way possible.

A woman's head-covering serves as a spiritual reminder, to help her remember spiritual messages. Every time a woman puts something on her head, she is reminded of G-d above her, running the world and helping her all the time. A man wears a yarmulke on his head for the same reason. The Yiddish word "*yarmulke*" is made up of the two Hebrew words, "*yarei malchus*"—one who fears the Kingship of Heaven.

The obligation to cover one's hair appears in the Torah portion of *Naso*. This portion deals with matters pertaining to the *ishah sotah*," a married woman whose husband suspects her of having been with another man. She must go to the Beis HaMikdash, the Holy Temple, where she is given bitter water to drink. If she is innocent, nothing happens. However, if she is guilty, she suffers an unnatural death.

In order to ascertain whether the woman was unfaithful to her husband, she is given water in which the Name of G-d was erased. In order to avoid erasing the Name, various actions are taken first to try and break the woman's haughty, brazen spirit. As a last resort, the *kohein* takes her in front of the Sanctuary, removes her head-covering, and makes her hair wild. From this, we learn that up until that moment, her hair was covered (*Ibn Ezra*, Bamidbar 5:18), and that exposed hair is considered a humiliation for a married woman (Rashi, *Kesubos* 2). Exposing her hair places the woman in a state of unparalleled humiliation and shame.

"And so we find with a *sotah*, that they measure her with the measure through which she measured. She stood at the doorway of her house to be seen by [the adulterer]; therefore, the *kohein* stands her up at the Nikanor Gate and reveals her shame to all. She spread attractive kerchiefs on her head for him; therefore, the *kohein* takes the covering off her head and places it at her feet" (*Sotah* 8b). If she was, indeed, with another man, or if she was unduly close to him, the first thing she probably did when trying to seduce him was to take off her head-covering.

"And why did [the *kohein*] make her hair wild? Because it is the way of Jewish women to cover their hair; therefore, he would make her hair wild and tell her, 'You strayed from the ways of the daughters of Israel, whose custom is to cover their hair, and went in the way of the gentiles, who walk around with loose hair. Now you have what you wanted...' " (*Bamidbar Rabbah* 9:16). Hair symbolizes the imagination: a state in which there are no boundaries and the evil inclination is free to act with madness. The *sotah* has strayed from the correct path. Instead of safeguarding the boundaries of her true inner world, she allowed herself to be drawn into a false, external one. Therefore, she is punished with the uncovering of her hair—a symbol of the world of falsehood.

A Jewish man, including one's husband, is forbidden to say holy words in the presence of a married woman whose hair is uncovered (*Shulchan Aruch, Orach Chaim* 75). Words of Torah and prayer may not be uttered in the presence of exposed parts of the body that ought to be covered and concealed. We learn this from the verse "And so your camp shall be holy" (Devarim 23:15). Therefore, even in her own home, a woman should fully cover her hair. In this merit, she will be blessed with the realization of the verse, "Your children shall be like olive shoots surrounding your table" (Tehillim 128:3).

"A woman should be modest and out of the limelight, in the

corner of her home. In this merit, it is said of her, 'Your children shall be like olive shoots.' Just as the olive tree does not shed its leaves neither in winter nor in summer, and is thus considered the most honored among trees, so will her children be great among people. Moreover, her husband will be showered with blessings from above and blessings from below, with wealth and children and grandchildren. It is of this that it is said, 'Behold, so will the G-d-fearing man be blessed' " (*Zohar*, *Parashas Naso* 126a).

"When she conducts herself according to '*das Yehudis*,' and is modest, she will merit having children who will be students of Scripture, students of Mishnah and doers of good deeds—as it says, 'Your children shall be like olive shoots'" (*Bamidbar Rabbah* 8).

Women are the source of blessing, and blessing comes only from things that are hidden from the eye (*Ta'anis* 8b). A woman who covers her hair is promised endless blessing. She merits a tremendous reward for everything that she sacrifices for the sake of Heaven. Sometimes the reward is a private thing, known only to her; and sometimes, it will be revealed to her only in the World to Come. On the occasions when the reward is public and apparent for all to see, it gives rise to a *kiddush Hashem*, the sanctification of G-d's Name.

> *In his early days, Rabbi Akiva was an ignorant man. He used to tend Kalba Savua's flocks at the time when Rachel, Kalba Savua's daughter, decided to marry him (Pesachim 49b). She perceived in him lofty spiritual strength therefore she made this decision (Ketubos 62b). In doing so, she gave up a life of wealth and luxury that she had in her father's home, in exchange for one of extreme poverty. Akiva and Rachel were so poor that they could not even allow themselves to purchase a bed to sleep on. Instead, they slept on a mat of straw and covered themselves with more straw. When they woke up in the morning, they had to pluck straw from their hair.*

One day, the Prophet Eliyahu came to them in the guise of a poor man, and asked for a bit of straw for his wife, who was about to give birth. The knowledge that there were people in the world even more destitute than they helped Akiva and Rachel to rejoice in their lot (Nedarim 50a).

Rachel would sell the plaits of her hair (some say the expensive kerchief that she wore on her head) and give Akiva the money she earned so that he could learn Torah and toil in it (Talmud Yerushalmi, Shabbos 6:1). She herself was satisfied with a simple head covering.

Akiva was stunned by his wife's enormous capacity for self-sacrifice. She had left behind a life of wealth and luxury and was now so poor that she had to pick straws out of her hair when she got up in the morning. He blessed her, and promised her that one day he would buy her a gold ornament for her head—a beautiful and costly piece of jewelry fashioned in the shape of a tiara (Tosafos, Shabbos 59a). Both his blessing and his promise came true.

Why did Rabbi Akiva promise her this? Was Rachel interested in elegant ornaments? Hadn't she willingly turned her back on a life of luxury in her father's house? Though Rabbi Akiva did become wealthy at a later stage of his life, at that point he was completely destitute!

In the era of the holy *Tanna'im*, when a scholar received ordination a golden cloak was spread over him. This was done in order to encourage and motivate the students to achieve this level, and to raise the honor of the Torah in the people's estimation (*Bava Metzia* 85a).

In promising her this unique and valuable ornament, Rabbi Akiva was essentially telling Rachel: "You sacrificed so much for my sake! Everything that I have is due to you. With Hashem's help, I will achieve commensurate with what you have invested in me, and you will be proud of me. In your merit, I will become a Torah scholar of such stature that I will be worthy of a special golden adornment. But instead of placing it on my own head—I will give *you* a golden ornament, and you will wear it on your head."

Rabbi Akiva wished to give his wife this expensive, golden ornament so that all women would see that a man's spiritual growth comes about in his wife's merit. Rabbi Akiva resolved that, unlike all the other scholars who had a golden cloak spread over them, he would not have this done to him. Instead, he would give his wife an ornament of gold. This ornament would ride on her head as a sign of appreciation for her sacrificing her hair (selling her beautiful head covering) only so that her husband could learn Torah.

When the time came, and Akiva had become "Rabbi Akiva," he gave his wife a *Yerushalayim shel zahav*, "Jerusalem of gold" tiara, as he'd promised her so long before. He instructed Rachel to walk out in public wearing the golden tiara on her head. On it was etched a picture of Jerusalem, the place from which Torah emanates. Rabbi Akiva's students were surprised to see his wife wearing such a valuable ornament. Rabbi Akiva responded by telling them that she deserved this ornament because of the sacrifice that she had made for Torah: "She has suffered greatly with me in the Torah" (*Avos D'Rabbi Nosson*, ch. 6).

Rabban Gamliel's wife asked her husband why he too hadn't given her the kind of ornament that Rachel received. She was not complaining about a lack of jewelry, as Rabban Gamliel, the *nasi*, leader of Israel, was extremely wealthy, and she undoubtedly could have bought herself a similar ornament had she wished. What she was asking was why her husband hadn't seen fit to bestow such an ornament upon her, the way Rabbi Akiva had seen fit to bestow one on his wife, Rachel. Rabban Gamliel replied that Rabbi Akiva and Rachel were on a higher level than the two of them—precisely because of something that the eye might perceive as a disadvantage.

"Rabbi Akiva and Rachel lived a Torah life in poverty, while we lived a Torah life amid riches," he told her. "Had you done what Rachel did, I would be as great in Torah as Rabbi Akiva. But you were not required to live in a hut, sell your hair (your expensive head covering), or sleep on a mat of straw. That is why I have not reached Rabbi Akiva's level—and why you did not merit the same symbol of outstanding excellence as his wife did" (Talmud Yerushalmi, *Shabbos* 6:1).

For many women, their hair is the crowning glory of their beauty. A woman who is willing to sacrifice her desire to look beautiful in order to do what is right in G-d's eyes will undoubtedly merit a spiritual bounty. Rachel illuminated all future generations with the personal example that she set. Shouldn't we all try to go in her way?

Chapter 10

The Additional Challenge

"Excuse me," an older woman addressed Michal.

Michal gave the woman a questioning look. Did she know her from somewhere? A friend of her mother's, perhaps, or a distant relative?

"I couldn't help noticing you when you walked into the store," the older woman continued. "Would you mind telling me your name? I have a nephew that I think would be a perfect match for you!"

"Uh..." Michal stammered, "I'm, uh, already married."

The woman stepped back in shock. "Your wig looks so natural!" she exclaimed. "I never would have guessed."

Michal nodded her head in embarrassment. All she wanted to do was escape as quickly as possible. This was the second match that she'd been offered since her marriage!

Nechama enjoyed her job as a secretary in a large firm, but there was one thing that greatly disturbed her. One of her coworkers was constantly trying to start a conversation with her, completely ignoring her efforts to slip away. Even though she tried to avoid any contact with him at all, he wouldn't leave her alone.

Nechama was growing more and more frustrated with what was rapidly becoming an intolerable situation for her. Finally she decided to be direct. "Why do you keep on bothering me?" she asked, the next time he sauntered over to her desk.

"It's… because of your hair!" the man blurted.

Nechama swallowed with difficulty, and unwittingly lifted a hand to touch her long, natural-looking wig. She really had nothing to say….

A married woman's hair is considered *ervah*, a kind of nakedness (*Berachos* 24a), which is why she is obligated to cover it. Choosing a suitable head-covering is a challenge all on its own. There are a variety of possibilities open to her, from which she may choose the covering that suits her taste and her personal style. At the same time, she must remember at all times that, like every other item of clothing, the item that covers her hair must be modest and not eye-catching.

There are women whose families or social circles have the custom to cover their hair with a kerchief or hat, while others have the custom to wear a wig. The halachic authorities who permit a married woman to cover her hair with a wig do so on condition that the look of the wig testifies to the fact that its wearer is covering her hair and not walking around bare-headed, like a single girl. In addition the wig must adhere to defined guidelines of modesty (see chapter 14).

It was a month before her wedding. Miriam sat in the wig salon, waiting her turn and thumbing through a catalogue that the stylist had thrust into her hands when she'd walked in. "Take a look through here," the stylist recommended. "Look at the pictures and try to imagine which styles would suit you. That will make it easier for you to decide how you want your wig to look."

Something was bothering Miriam. She felt as if she were facing an important trial but she wasn't sure that she was ready to stand up to it successfully.

Now that she was preparing to build a home of her own, was this the time to change her priorities? As a married woman, did she want to be constantly concerned with her external appearance and worry more about how she looked in public than she had done when she was single? Was it her obligation to suit her style to the gentile women pictured in the catalogue? Would she too be tossing her head from side to side to keep the wig hair out of her eyes?

The Chazon Ish said that the measure of a women's fear of Heaven is gauged by how she covers her hair (*Pe'er Hador*, part 3, p. 18). In the same way that a woman must be careful to keep her clothes, *begadeha*, from turning into her traitors, *bogdeha*, she is obliged to use her *binah yeseirah*—that special, extra dimension of wisdom with which she's been endowed—and must be careful with regard to her head-covering. She has to be honest with herself and check to see if her head-covering complies with the rules of modesty.

Starting at a young age, every girl dreams of marrying one day. As she grows older, those dreams become more defined. They attain a tangible dimension. Among other things, she pictures the kind of head-covering that will become a part of her after she marries. Every young woman needs to test herself: Does she long to cover her hair in order to fulfill G-d's commandment and be more modest—or is she waiting for the moment when she can don a glorious wig and look even more beautiful than she looked with her natural hair?

If a woman wore her wig only in front of her husband, there would be no problem at all. However, usually the woman knows that many other men are destined to see her in the wig that she chooses. This fact turns her choice of a wig into a real problem and one that requires thought. Understanding the problem, though, is half the solution.

The wig-making industry worldwide manufactures wigs for a double purpose: First, wigs are used to enhance the outward appearance and help people change their image at will. For example, wigs are used extensively in the entertainment industry. Second, wigs are used by people who are ill, Heaven forbid, and whose hair has fallen out. For these people, the use of a wig helps them retain their natural appearance.

The same wig-making industry services the Torah-observant community as well. Jewish women who cover their hair for reasons of modesty constitute only a small percentage of wig-buying customers in the world, which means that they end up purchasing wigs that were initially intended for other purposes. Wig manufacturers do not take into consideration at all the Jewish laws of modesty. Their only interest—like most business people—is in reaping profits from the wigs they produce. It is easy to understand, then, that each wig must be inspected very critically.

When we purchase an item that we plan to use in the way it was intended to be used, we can rely to a certain extent on the manufacturer, and on the broad spectrum of consumers who bought it before us and found it suitable to the purpose for which it was designed. However, when we buy an object that was intended for a different purpose than the one for which we will be using it, we must be doubly careful to see if the item is in fact suitable to our needs. The fact that many have purchased it before us and were satisfied with the way it served their purpose is no indication to us either way.

When a woman is about to buy a wig, the first thing she has to do is keep her eye on the reason she's planning to buy it: the mitzvah of covering her hair. Understanding the importance of this mitzvah will help direct her to choosing a more modest wig. Being scrupulous with the modesty of our clothes in general is a challenge for any Jewish woman—but wigs pose the greatest challenge of all .

The stylist was busy styling Ruthie's new wig. The steep price tag was making a serious and painful dent in the family budget, but Ruthie was prepared to pay any price to feel pretty. Nevertheless, she was determined not to compromise on the demands of Jewish law.

Ruthie showed the stylist a pamphlet that her husband had brought home on the subject of modesty in wigs, and pointed to the section about wig length. Ruthie really wanted her wig to conform to all the rules listed in the pamphlet. But it was so hard. With each snip of the scissors and the loss of another silky, gorgeous lock of "hair," she waved good-bye to more of the hard-earned dollars that she'd struggled to save in order to buy this wig….

"You surely don't want me to make it any shorter than this!" the stylist exclaimed, breaking into Ruthie's feverish thoughts. "You look simply stunning! If I cut off any more, it'll ruin the whole effect!"

Ruthie's eyes filled with tears. This trial is too hard for me, she thought. Somehow, though, she managed to muster the necessary strength.

"Go on cutting, please," she said firmly.

Wigs arrive from the manufacturer long and beautiful. Cutting them means a great deal of money down the drain. A woman seated in the stylist's chair in the wig salon will find it difficult indeed to throw away precious centimeters of such an expensive item, while at the same time giving up the lovely look that long hair provides. This is a genuine hardship that cannot be lightly dismissed.

To overcome this hardship, a woman needs knowledge to act as a counter-force and help her weigh the matter in the light of reason. The moment women understand that they are prohibited from dressing in a manner that attracts men, all that remains is to learn what attracts them. The better they understand this topic, the easier it will be for them to choose wigs that conceal their femininity and not, Heaven forbid, those that will accentuate and emphasize it. This is an additional challenge for a woman—but one that she can certainly meet.

It is impermissible to wear a wig that looks completely natural. It is not enough that, "Everyone knows that it's a wig!" The wig stylist cannot be the one to decide whether or not a wig is provocative or alluring. The rules that our Torah leaders have established for wigs are the only source we can rely on, and they are there to assist women when making this crucial decision.

The halachic opinions that permit the wearing of wigs were talking about wigs that were short, unnatural-looking, and "wiggy." Such wigs were in use a century ago, explains Maran HaGaon Rav Yosef Sholom Elyashiv, *shlita*. They were short and stiff, and the hairs did not move from their place. Therefore, they were neither provocative nor alluring. In contrast, a wig that is long, free-flowing, and natural-looking does not constitute a modest head-covering. The question that a woman must ask herself as she visits the wig salon is this: Does this wig effectively conceal my femininity, or does it show and emphasize it? When we take into account what hair symbolizes, we must check to see if the wigs that are in such widespread use today do in fact fulfill their purpose adequately.

Until now, we've been dealing with the style and appearance of the wig. Another factor that must be taken into consideration is the hair from which the wig was made. In order for a wig to be permissible to wear, it must be made from "kosher" hair—that is, hair that was never used in any sort of rite or ritual connected with *avodah zarah*, idol worship. It's important to note that the "kosher" stamp applies only to the hair from which a particular wig was made, and does not attest at all to the modesty of the wig itself.

Of course, wigs are not the only permissible form of head-covering, and some women prefer a different form. One of the things that may have influenced their decision is the fact that wigs must meet so many criteria. Also, it's not easy to find wigs nowadays that are non-natural, short, and rigid (and it is doubtful how many women would want to wear them, even if they were readily available). Of course, even if a woman chooses to cover her hair with a kerchief or hat, she must make sure that her head-covering is modest and that it fulfills the purpose for which it is being worn.

A woman may worry—needlessly—that there could be something immodest in her standing out as the only woman wearing a kerchief among a crowd of others in wigs. This is absolutely not a concern. Such a woman would be no different than a modestly dressed one in a crowd of people who are not modestly dressed. Certainly, both of these women are sanctifying G-d's Name with their appearance, despite their standing out by being different from the others.

By blindly following what "everybody" is doing, one can be mislead. Our only sure bet is following the ways set down by the

Torah luminaries that G-d has placed in our generation. The *posek hador*, our generation's great halachic authority, Maran Rav Yosef Sholom Elyashiv, *shlita*, has clearly stated that in his opinion it is preferable for a woman to cover her hair with a kerchief rather than a wig. He constantly expresses his concern about the use of wigs that are not modest—a practice which, he says, has made inroads even into the families of pious men and *roshei yeshivah*.

Maran Rav Shlomo Zalman Auerbach, *zt"l*, expressed the same concern. As he once put it to Rav Dan Segal, *shlita*: "They cover their hair, and then make every effort to make it look uncovered. Therefore, in my opinion this is a loathsome thing. But who can we talk to?" He also said that, when Mashiach comes, the first thing he'll do is abolish the use of wigs (as quoted by his son-in-law, *shlita*). Many halachic authorities and Torah scholars in our time agree with this approach.

> *What an amazing article! Chava thought, leaning back on the sofa. What she'd just read had stunned her. There had been truth shining forth from every word.... But that didn't mean that she planned to change anything in a practical sense. After all, what would "everybody" say? The opinions of any number of faces that she saw in her mind's eye created an impassable barrier in her mind.*
>
> *After giving it some thought, however, she decided that she had to try—if only to prove to herself that it was impossible for her to wear a kerchief instead of a wig. Thus she resolved to wear a kerchief to the parent-teacher conference the following week.*
>
> *On the night in question, Chava stood in front of the mirror and studied her reflection. An inner weakness assailed her. "Have I gone mad?" she asked herself. But she wasn't the type of person to back away from a decision. She took a deep breath and left her house.*

The minute she entered the school building, Chava felt herself blushing. She saw the looks that were sent her way, and heard the whispers behind her back. "Did I do the right thing?" she wondered, as her tension increased. "This is just too hard—even on a one-time trial basis!"

She paced to and fro in the corridor between the classrooms. She felt as if her self-image had just been shattered into tiny pieces. A real identity crisis.

"Relax," said a small, inner voice. "It's still you."

She had chosen an enormous challenge—a challenge linked to her hair, her brain, and to the root of her soul, the highest part of her being.

As she stood chatting with other mothers waiting in line to speak to the teachers, she felt the bewilderment that had engulfed her lifting. By the time her turn came to meet the teacher, her self-confidence had returned. On the way home, she smiled to herself. The ordeal by fire was behind her.

The strength that Chava gained from that evening gave her the encouragement to try again and again.

Some time passed since her first try at appearing in public in a kerchief. Occasionally, someone still asks her, "Did you really put your wig away in the cupboard for good? You used to look so beautiful in it!"

"I'm just trying to see how one gets along without it," Chava answers with a bashful smile. In all honesty, she does not yet have a decisive answer to that question.

Every woman is destined to be rewarded for her desire to grow. She is basically in the place where her thoughts are right now. As Rabbi Tzaddok HaKohein of Lublin wrote, "Where a person's thoughts are, there the entire person is—for the essence of a person is not his body, but his soul" (*Tzidkas HaTzaddik* 144). G-d knows what her thoughts are, and He will surely reward her for her efforts. Even when her efforts and attempts do not lead to any real achievement, they do not leave her empty-handed.

Growth is not a matter of "all or nothing." Every person is different, in terms of their personal makeup, background, and environment. Every woman has to do her utmost to improve at her own pace.

It wasn't easy, but Shoshana decided to trade her wig for a kerchief. Gradually she began wearing a kerchief on her head when she went out to run errands and other places, slowly getting accustomed to the change.

Until she received the invitation.

How, she wondered gloomily as she held the printed invitation in her hand, could she possibly attend a bar mitzvah on Shabbos wearing a kerchief? There would be so many people participating in the affair. Basically, the whole neighborhood would be there. The prospect of being the only woman in attendance not wearing a wig was daunting.

The Shabbos in question arrived. Shoshana put the kerchief on her head and took a deep breath before facing the crowd. She entered the shul hall and made her way through the crowd to offer her good wishes to the bar mitzvah boy's mother. All the way there, she felt the other women's eyes on her. Some of them stared, others looked shocked, and there were a few who giggled.

"Why are you wearing that rag on your head?" a friend asked her. Now Shoshana was sure that she hadn't imagined the reactions. Had she undertaken something too large for her narrow shoulders? She suddenly felt very unsure of herself. She was bewildered but despite her inner quaking, she pasted a smile on her face and tried to pretend that her friend's question hadn't affected her at all.

After she joined some other women sitting at a table, she

managed to forget for a few minutes that she was the only one among them wearing a kerchief. Suddenly, an old friend whom she hadn't seen in ages was sitting by her side. "Don't you think you're attracting a little too much attention?" her friend asked.

The words stung. Shoshana cringed inwardly, and fought back a tear that was threatening to fall. Then she answered simply, "I went personally to ask the posek hador, halachic authority of the generation, Rav Elyashiv, shlita. And he told me that it's preferable to wear a kerchief. I'm only trying to see if I can manage without my wig."

The moment the words were out of her mouth, Shoshana could have kicked herself. Why hadn't she responded with confidence and pride? How absurd, to feel that she had to defend herself and justify her decision! She comforted herself with the encouraging looks she thought she saw in eyes of a few of her friends, who, though wearing wigs like everyone else there, seemed to respect her decision even if they didn't say so out loud.

When it was time to go home, Shoshana heaved a sigh of relief. Her husband met her in front of the hall, and his look of compassion and pride was all she needed. It gave her strength and reminded her that she had to do what she believed to be right, and not be afraid of everyone else's opinion. As they went home together, she felt as if a pleasant glow enveloped her head. She'd done it. She had performed an act of self-sacrifice for the sake of a mitzvah.

Deep down inside, she knew that Hashem was happy with the effort she'd made. She thanked Him for helping her through the ordeal, and silently asked Him to help her again, because on her refrigerator at home hung another invitation.

Her cousin was getting married in two weeks' time and she was determined to try again.

It certainly couldn't be any worse, she thought to herself.

Being different is not easy. Even worse, the *yetzer hara*, evil inclination, is likely to try to convince us that being different is arrogant and conceited. In actuality, any woman who wears a kerchief instead of a wig will tell you that arrogance had no part to play in her decision.

Once a woman has passed the social barrier, those closest to her will grow accustomed to her appearance. They will stop making comments about her new head-covering. She too will become used to the new look that she sees in the mirror, and will begin identifying with it more and more.

There will still be days when doubts arise in her heart. "Doesn't a wig cover my hair better than a kerchief?" The solution to this is to be aware and make sure that her kerchief always covers all of her hair. This is no impossible feat: our mothers did it for thousands of years.

"Perhaps it's not respectable-looking?" This, too, is a question that may trouble her at times. The truth is, feeling respectable is a question of what one is used to. A woman who is accustomed to wearing a kerchief on her head will accept herself that way and feel respectable. Were all women to cover their hair with kerchiefs, it would not occur to anyone that there might be any inherent lack of respectability in doing so.

Naomi was in turmoil. The night before, she'd met her good friend, Tzira, at a wedding—and what a shock! On Tzira's head was a kerchief, tied with charming simplicity.

Anger bubbled up inside Naomi. What a betrayal! Tzira was a young woman of her own age, and she'd appeared in public—at a wedding, no less!—wearing a kerchief instead of her pretty wig. Naomi felt terrible. She felt as if Tzira had abandoned her.

Why did this bother her so much? Naomi tried to figure it out as she combed her own lovely wig. She ran her fingers through the hair that framed her face so perfectly, and looked in the mirror. "Tzira has done what I can't do," she finally confessed to her reflection. "She's done what I'm not prepared to do."

Naomi loved the time she spent in the wig salon, as the stylist pampered her wig. She always felt so good when she left that place! Until recently, Tzira had felt the same way. What had led her to make the change?

Naomi decided to find out.

Modesty is linked to external appearance, and it requires us to put our minds in control of how we look. Excessive focus on one's outward appearance can turn into a form of idol worship. This is what modesty is intended to prevent. Beauty, as a value, is secondary in importance to the value of holiness. When beauty serves holiness, it enhances it; but when beauty becomes the master, it turns into a tyrant. The Torah directs a Jew to steer away from being overly involved with the outside aspect of life, the *panim*, face, and to focus more on the spiritual and the inward, the *penim*, inside.

Today, we are not enslaved physically, but we are chained to the edicts that society places upon us. Nevertheless, we have the ability to free ourselves gradually, step by step, from these chains. All it takes is a genuine desire to liberate ourselves and be free from the non-Torah influences of society.

True freedom comes when we learn to subdue our desires and passions. The way to accomplish this is by following the path carved out for us by our forefathers, and to sincerely and wholeheartedly believe that we have the power to withstand the trials and overcome them. G-d will give us the strength and the courage to do what is right and good in His eyes. And then our nation will be blessed with peace, as it says, "G-d will give His nation strength; G-d will bless His nation with peace" (Tehillim 29:11).

To improve and strengthen our modesty—is there a better way for women, the pillar of their homes, to influence their families and the entire Jewish people?

Chapter 11

Especially for Husbands

The marriage bond is the most exalted connection that can exist between two human beings. Husband and wife become a single entity—two halves of a whole, as it says, "And they shall be as one flesh" (Bereishis 2:24). Since a woman is a part of her husband—"His wife is like his own self" (*Berachos* 24a)—it is obvious that he would not wish to share her with others. A woman's femininity was given to her for her to express only to her own husband. "And Elkanah knew Chana, his wife" (I Shmuel 1:19); only a husband really knows his wife, and it is this unique facet that strengthens the special bond and covenant between them.

A wife is permitted to her husband and forbidden to everyone else. When a man sees other men eyeing his wife, he should cringe inside. His very soul should recoil. Some of the Divine abundance that his wife receives from him is being lost, and this is truly tragic.

When husband and wife are together, the woman is the recipient of a Divine abundance, *shefah*, that G-d gives her through her husband. The man gives his wife half of the life force that has been granted to him. In the merit of this giving, the source of his own vitality is renewed (*Tomer Devorah*, ch. 9).

A man is compared to the soul and his wife to the body. At such times, the body receives vitality from the soul. The woman's soul attains a sense of unity and her life is suffused with an inner peace (*Zohar*, *Vayeshev* 181:2). This time is called *shtiyah*, drinking, because it nourishes the woman like food and drink (*Nedarim* 20b; *Kesubos* 65b).

When a man thinks about a woman who is not his wife, the *sitra achra*, the negative forces, open that woman's reservoir of abundance and start bringing it down through that man. Such a situation destroys the bond between husband and wife. In essence, he is "stealing" the vitality that the woman was meant to receive from her husband. In addition, "One who looks at women, even if he does not mean to transgress, Heaven forbid, ends up with an image etched in his mind, which will damage his own soul" (*Midbar Kadmos LeChidah*). Though no actual deed was done, the thought alone steals the abundance that belongs to the woman, causing it to come down through the man who looked at her. And, as is well known, "Thoughts of sin are more injurious than sin itself" (*Yoma* 29a).

When a woman's abundance is stolen by another man, her life is damaged and she does not receive her true vitality from her husband. And when a man thinks about a woman who is not his wife, this causes him to give *his* wife the abundance of another woman that came down to the world through him. Thus, his wife does not receive the life force that G-d designated for her, and she will feel the lack.

The modest woman merits being the recipient of her true abundance and enjoys complete satisfaction in all areas of her life. Therefore, she has no need for attention from strangers. "Modesty is beautiful" (*Bamidbar Rabbah* 1:3); "There is nothing more beloved by G-d than modesty" (*Pesikta* 46:1). In modesty, then, there is both beauty and affection. When a woman is modest, both she and her husband can feel the genuine abundance passing between them in a wholesome and correct way; therefore, the bond between them is whole. The word for "affection"—*chibah*—and one of G-d's Names, spelled *yud* and *heh*, have the same numerical value: 15. This offers a hint and is a sign that the *Shechinah*, Divine Presence, resides with a couple where affection abides between them.

When a man knows that his wife is reserved especially and exclusively for him, the bond they share is elevated to a place that belongs only to the two of them. "Gladden the beloved companions as You gladdened Your creature in the Garden of Eden from aforetime" (from the *sheva berachos* blessings). The two of them feel as if they are the only man and woman in the world. The more the woman conceals herself from other men, the more special and strong the bond between them.

When a woman dresses modestly and conducts herself modestly, she gives her husband the message that she is saving her feminine essence especially for him. In this way, his love for her grows, because every man wants a faithful wife. When men don't understand the principles of modesty, they are liable to mistakenly encourage the wrong things.

> *Yossi was at a loss. His wife had just bought herself a new skirt and blouse. "How do I look?" she asked.*
>
> *Yossi was no expert on women's fashions, but even he could see that the skirt was too short and the neckline of the blouse too wide. He was certain that it was not right*

for other men to see his wife this way. But how to tell this to her, without hurting her feelings? She came from a very religiously observant family, so she would undoubtedly claim that she knew what was permitted and what was forbidden. After all, her clothes were her own personal business, weren't they?

Because the issue was not sufficiently clear to him, and because he did not know what the correct thing to do was, Yossi did not express his feelings. With an artificial smile he mumbled that she looked all right.

It is a husband's obligation to draw the lines in the home. The author of the *Peleh Yoetz* defines this as part and parcel of a man's obligation to love his wife: "And the primary love is spiritual love, and it is his obligation to reprimand her gently and to guide her in the ways of modesty" (*Erech Ahavat Ish VeIshah*). When the husband is a *ben Torah*, it is that much more incumbent upon him to establish the home's spiritual level. If necessary, when he has reservations about his wife's mode of dress, he must express these reservations clearly.

Sometimes a man senses that there is something amiss with what his wife is wearing, but he can't put his finger on it. Or it can happen that he becomes so accustomed to seeing her dress a certain way that he doesn't even perceive a problem with her appearance. As a result, his sensitivity toward her dress is diminished—so that, when his heart tells him that she is not dressed properly, he tends to ignore the feeling or assumes that he's being overly sensitive. Frequently, he simply lacks the practical knowledge to correct the situation.

"Well? How do you like it?" Ahuva asked eagerly.

"You...look...beautiful." Her husband's answer came slowly.

Ahuva smiled. She'd just bought herself a new wig in honor of her brother's upcoming wedding, and she thought she looked terrific in it.

But Shaul, her husband, wasn't smiling. Something was bothering him, though he couldn't put his finger on what, exactly, it was. A troubling thought kept nagging at his brain. Studying the flowing, well-styled wig again, he suddenly realized what was troubling him. More than once, as he'd walked along the street, his eye had been caught by just this kind of wig on the heads of other women, before he'd had time to avert his gaze. Who was his wife trying to look so beautiful for?

"Are… are you sure it's not too long?" he asked tentatively.

"Oh, no." Ahuva sounded very certain. "My stylist tells me that plenty of women are wearing wigs that are much longer than this!"

Yes, Shaul thought. I've seen them.

Shaul didn't know what to do. He felt angry at the mere thought of all those strange men seeing his wife in all her glory. He couldn't possibly understand why it was permissible to wear such wigs—but he'd never heard explicit instructions on this matter.

The Vilna Gaon says that men were commanded to invest their energies in Torah study, and women were commanded to invest their energies in modesty. "For this is the whole purpose of man…. The evil inclination lies in wait, and his *yetzer* tries to exert control…. The antidote, for men, is involvement in Torah study, and for women, modesty and working on character traits and ethics." *(Iggeres HaGra, HaNusach HaMeduyak, Aram Tzovah* 5626).

Modesty is a challenge that accompanies women throughout their lives, the way Torah study accompanies men. Just as the efforts that a man exerts in learning Torah influence the degree of holy abundance that will pour down onto every area of his life, the same applies to the efforts that a woman puts into her modesty.

But for a woman to succeed in recruiting her strength and investing effort in the area of modesty, she needs her husband's help.

His encouragement is critical in this area, because every woman wants to find favor in her husband's eyes. A man should constantly express his love and appreciation to his wife, and repeatedly assure her that she always finds favor in his eyes. This poses no great challenge for men; our Sages tell us that, in the nature of things, "A wife appears favorable to her husband" (*Sotah* 47a). The moment a woman becomes aware of the principle underlying her obligation to safeguard her modesty, and understands her own need to retain favor in her husband's eyes, it becomes much easier for her husband to explain gently why it would be inappropriate for her to wear certain clothes when in the presence of other people. If he links his message to a sincere compliment, it will be a lot easier for his wife to accept what he's saying.

The characteristics of a woman's femininity are so precious that she must take care to use them only when appropriate—that is, in her husband's company alone, and far from strange eyes. Therefore, an immodest appearance in front of others is always forbidden. A man who wants to show off his wife's beauty in front of his friends exhibits his complete ignorance of the very essence of married life. He certainly has no clue as to the damage this attitude is incurring for both of them.

Moreover, it is a big mistake to think that, because a woman should try to appear beautiful to her husband, she is permitted to do so in public. As the Chofetz Chaim, *zt"l*, wrote: "Do not let the evil inclination convince you that she will escape judgment because she had to adorn herself in front of her husband, lest she grow unappealing in his eyes. This is an error because that is something that belongs only in the home, and not in the marketplace" (*Geder Olam*, ch. 4).

Maran HaRav Eliezer Menachem Shach, *zt"l*, said that men's Torah study goes over to the side of evil when their wives dress immodestly. Rav Dan Segal, *shlita*, explains that religiously observant women who dress immodestly pose a greater trial for men than other women out there in the street.

"You shall not stray after your hearts and after your eyes" (Bamidbar 15:39). A man's thoughts bring him to the place where his thoughts reside, and his eyes bring him to the place at which he is looking. The numerical values of the word *re'iyah*, "sight," and the word *gevurah*, "strength," are identical. In his struggle with the *yetzer hara*, the evil inclination, a man's main strength lies in his sight, for that is the opening through which the *yetzer hara* gains entrance to him (*Ben Yehoyadah, Sotah* 8). The letters of *re'iyah* are also the same as in the word *yirah*, the Hebrew word for "fear." Sight is the most important of the human senses. A person has the power to shake off evil through exerting control over his sight, to help him attain fear of Heaven.

Neither a man nor his wife is in the position to decide which article of clothing is appropriate and which is not. Because people differ widely in their opinions of what constitutes modest attire and what does not, there exists a range too broad for interpretation. *Gedolei Yisrael*, our Torah leaders, have established guidelines in this area (see chapter 14). They have met the enormous challenges and trials of our generation and have set down binding rules for modest clothing. Therefore, men and women alike must obey the words of today's leaders of the Torah world, even if they do not understand them. As our Sages have taught regarding the verse: "You shall be careful to do according to everything that they will teach you.... And you shall not deviate from the word that they will tell you, right or left" (Devarim 17:10–11) —"even if they tell you that your right is your left, and your left is your right!"

This is the meaning of *emunas chachamim*, belief in our Sages. This is how we submit ourselves to G-d and accept upon ourselves the yoke of Heaven. Therefore, modesty is an expression of *emunah*, our belief.

"A woman who fears G-d, she should be praised" (Mishlei 31:30). Our strong character, which serves as a model for others, and our ability to do the right thing in G-d's eyes, will afford us peace of mind in this world—and endless reward in the World to Come.

The Gemara tells the story of Rav Bana'ah, an amora who lived about 2,000 years ago, and who traveled around Eretz Yisrael identifying the graves of tzaddikim. When he reached Me'aras HaMachpelah, the Cave of the Patriarchs, he went inside and saw Avraham and Sarah. Sarah was "peering at her husband's head" (*Bava Basra* 58a).

Our patriarch, Avraham, performed mighty deeds in building the Jewish nation together with his wife, Sarah. They achieved all this within the framework of their married life. There was Avraham, and there was Sarah—but, in the end, they combined into a single entity. Sarah's "peering at her husband's head" may be understood to indicate that a wife's primary task is to check her husband's thoughts and character traits. She does so using her *binah yeseirah*, a special dimension of wisdom that G-d has granted her. The husband who comprehends the gift that was given to both of them will appreciate it, knowing that it is for his benefit as well.

The author of the *Tiferes Shlomo* shines a new light on G-d's instruction to Avraham to listen to his wife: "*Shema b'kolah.*" A man who appreciates his wife and listens to what she says will hear *Keriyas Shema* in her words—the verse that betokens our acceptance of Heaven's yoke. The world around us is intent on shrugging the yoke of Heaven off its shoulders. In contrast, the voice of a Jewish wife contain the declaration "*Shema Yisrael!*" She enables a perpetual acceptance of Heaven's yoke in her home. "There is no limit to a good woman's goodness" (*Midrash Shocher Tov* 59:2).

After our nation received the Torah, G-d instructed Moshe to teach the people what to do next. One might assume that, after such a momentous and uplifting event, Moshe would have directed the people toward exalted actions. Perhaps he'd have the men stay up all that night, learning the Torah they'd just received. Or maybe they'd be instructed to joyously celebrate the giving of the Torah. But the Torah tells us of a different instruction: "Go tell them, 'Return to your tents'" (Devarim 5:27). Rashi explains that the men were told to go back to their wives. For the three days prior to the giving of the Torah, the men had been ordered to separate from their wives; now it was time to return to them.

A man needs a wife. He received a gift, as it says, "A good woman is a wonderful gift.... She is given into the embrace of a G-d-fearing man" (*Yevamos* 63b). Receiving the Torah is something that needs to be done in unity, as with Avraham and Sarah.

A woman's traits are compared to those of honey. As Maran HaGaon Rav Elyashiv, *shlita*, points out, the numerical value of *ishah*, "woman," is equivalent to that of *d'vash*, "honey": both words equal 306. He explains that this hints at the Rosh's words, in the chapter "*Keitzad Mevarchin*": By rights, honey ought to be rendered impure by the bees' feet that are mixed into it. However, eating honey is permissible because of a special feature it possesses that allows it to neutralize the contaminants in the bees' feet. This feature allows the honey to actually absorb the bees' feet and turn them into honey as well. This is precisely a Jewish woman's strength: G-d has imbued her with character traits that have the power to neutralize the negative forces in her home and in her husband, even when those negativities have already gained entrance—just as honey neutralizes the impurity of the bees' feet after they've been introduced into it (HaRav Yitzchak Zilberstein, *shlita*, in *Aleinu l'Shabe'ach*).

Yanky and Miri were on their way to a family wedding. It had been some time since they'd both decided that Miri would try to wear a kerchief instead of a wig, which she was used to. And this was the first time since then that she'd had occasion to attend a wedding.

Yanky was anxious for her. All the women on both sides of their families wore wigs. When they reached the entrance to the wedding hall and Miri turned toward the women's side, his heart skipped a beat.

"Forward, march!" he said warmly. "I really admire the step you've taken. Just know, you look wonderful!"

And then, just before they parted, he whispered to her, "No one but me knows your true beauty, and I'm very proud of you."

Husbands are the ones who must make sure that their wives' outward appearance is a modest one, as well as encouraging their wives' growth in the mitzvah of modesty, despite the trials involved and despite the reactions of those around them. In the long run, they will both profit immeasurably. As the Chofetz Chaim writes: "The addition of every added precaution in modesty leads to increased Divine Presence, as well as greater security and protection against all troubles and prosecutors."

"A beautiful wife—fortunate is her husband; the number of his days is doubled" (*Yevamos* 63b). Rashi explains that such a man is happy in his life with his wife, and therefore feels as if he's been given double years of life. We can also interpret this to mean that a modest woman is beautiful in her husband's eyes. He receives all the abundance of her vitality, in order to pass it on to her; therefore, the years of his life are figuratively doubled.

How happy is the husband whose wife is interested in strengthening her modesty when in the company of other people. Is there any man who'd be prepared to forgo such happiness?

Chapter 12

Summary of the Laws of Yichud

Written by HaGaon HaRav Yitzchak Zilberstein, *shlita*

Definition of Yichud: The following constitutes *yichud*: When a man and a woman who are not married to each other are in a closed room, or any other place where they will not be disturbed. If a man or woman finds him- or herself in such a situation, he or she must leave the place as quickly as possible. If there is some doubt as to the situation, they must consult a halachic authority.

Situations that are not included in the prohibition of yichud:

- A man is permitted to be alone with his mother, his daughter, his grandmother, or his granddaughter.
- A woman is permitted to be alone with her father, her son, her grandfather, or her grandson.
- A brother and sister may be alone together for up to thirty days on a permanent basis.

The ages that apply to the prohibition of yichud:

- A man or boy aged 13 and older is not permitted to be alone with a woman or girl aged 3 and older.
- A woman or girl aged 12 and older is not permitted to be alone with a man or boy aged 9 and older.

Included in the prohibition of yichud are:

- An adopted son or daughter; extended-family relatives; male or female non-Jews; a bride and groom in the case of a *chuppas niddah*, in accordance with the laws of *taharat hamishpachah*; male or female babysitters; male or female doctors, and so on.

Solutions for Avoiding the Prohibition of Yichud

The following are some solutions for circumventing the prohibition of *yichud*. There is no *yichud* in the following situations:

1) When the room has an opening that faces a public thoroughfare. For example:

   a) The room has a door facing a public thoroughfare, and that door is unlocked. If people usually enter the room through that door without knocking, it is as if the door were not locked.

   b) The room has a window facing a public thoroughfare, so that the passersby in the street can see what is taking place inside the room.

In a car there is no prohibition of *yichud*, on condition the car is driving through an area where there are passersby at least every five minutes.

In an elevator there is no prohibition of *yichud* on condition that the ride does not last more than three minutes.

2) When the man and the woman are in two separate rooms, and one of the doors is locked. It is preferable that the key reside with the woman.

3) When there is a *shomer*, guard, present with them.

The following people can serve as guards:

a) A girl between the ages of 5 and 9, or a boy between the ages of 9 and 13.

b) The man's sister, daughter, mother, or grandmother.

c) The woman's brother, son, father or grandfather; the woman's mother-in-law, her mother-in-law's daughter, and her husband's daughter by another wife.

Where there are no passersby, two *shomrim*, guards, are necessary.

4) In a place where there are many men—A woman may be alone with two kosher men in a place where there are passersby. ("Kosher" means they are Torah observant people who fear Heaven, and about whom there is no reason to suspect laxity in the laws of modesty.) The custom in Sephardic communities is to allow *yichud* only when there are at least three kosher men and at least three women.

5) When his wife is with him—A woman may be alone with a Jew if his wife is with him in the same apartment.

6) When a woman's husband is in town—A woman may be alone with a man.

It is superfluous to mention how important it is to know the laws of *yichud* very well. Of course, since these are G-d's commandments, we must be scrupulous in observing them. But it is important to understand that these are especially crucial laws in day-to-day living, and being ignorant of them can lead to serious consequences.

> *Rabbi Berger couldn't fall asleep that night. This was the most difficult case he'd ever encountered in his life, and he was gravely concerned about serious future ramifications. Tomorrow, he was planning to discuss the matter with one of the leading Torah authorities of the generation.*
>
> *"How do things like this happen?" he asked himself sadly.*
>
> *His wife was awake, too. He shared his thoughts with her – without, of course, revealing the identities of the involved parties.*
>
> *"How could this have been prevented?" he asked her.*
>
> *"Simple," his wife replied. "Through scrupulous observance of the laws of yichud."*
>
> *Yes, the rabbi thought. This was the answer. Had these laws been carefully observed, such a thing could never have taken place. If only we all lived our lives being scrupulous about the laws that G-d has given us, how much pain and distress could be prevented....*

Which of us would not want to scrupulously observe the laws that G-d, in His compassion, has given us for our benefit?

Chapter 13

The Engaged Couple

Maran HaRav Schach, *zt"l*, was of the opinion that a couple's engagement should be no longer than three months' duration.

"Does the *rosh yeshivah* really mean that?" a certain rabbi once asked him.

"Do I mean it?" Rav Schach echoed, surprised at the other's incomprehension. "In actual fact, I believe it would be best if only three *hours* passed between the engagement and the wedding!"

Rav Schach transmitted a powerful message: The engagement period should be as short as possible. The shorter the period between the engagement and the wedding, the better.

The engagement period is a time of preparation for marriage in different ways: spiritually, emotionally, intellectually, and practically. It is not a time when the future bride and groom are meant to get to know each other in a deep way. During this period, they are as forbidden to one another as any man and woman who are unmarried.

An engaged couple is not permitted to behave as if they are married. All the laws of modesty and *yichud* apply to the couple during the period of their engagement. Even more so—during this period they need to behave with even greater modesty. Because they know that they are soon to become man and wife, they must take extra precautions in their behavior when they meet. For them, the less they meet each other during this period, the better. This will spare them the tension of feelings they may not express—a tension that can only lead to inevitable frustration, caused by their inability to give each other the kind of attention they wish they could give.

The first year of marriage will provide them with endless opportunities to get to know one another. Starting from their wedding, the *Shechinah*, Divine Presence, rests on the couple for the rest of their lives together, and they become two halves of a whole. However, in the period before the wedding, this covenant is not yet in existence. All that exists is the anticipation of the bond.

> *The engagement party was behind them. Shulamis looked eagerly at the large calendar above her desk. There were three months to go before the wedding.*
>
> *In her mind's eye, she imagined herself chatting on the phone with Chaim several times each day. It was going to be so nice! She also planned to meet him as often as possible. She had no doubt that she and Chaim would be as close as possible by the time the big day arrived.... That was what the engagement period was for, right?*
>
> *Fortunately, she was about to start taking kallah, bridal, classes the next day. Her kallah teacher would have to set her straight.*

From her perspective, a young girl may have a hard time understanding what damage could result from a ceaseless association between herself and her future husband. But she should accept the clear opinion of our great Torah leaders in this matter. G-d created man and woman as two different beings, and each is sometimes unable to see things from the other's point of view. Even though she can see no reason why she and her fiancé should not meet and speak to each other very frequently, she must understand that, for him, it is not desirable to see her too often at this stage.

She needs to accept this as a fact, and to recognize that, until the wedding, contact between them must be kept to a minimum. If they are both aware of this, it will be easier for them to limit their interactions during this period, without either of them feeling insulted. If they speak on the phone in accordance with an agreed-upon schedule, and meet only when necessary, neither of them will develop unrealistic expectations or feel disappointed when the other does not call on a frequent basis. The more organized their meeting and phoning schedule, the calmer they will be, and the more smoothly, with Heaven's help, their engagement period will pass.

The countdown to the wedding can be an emotional time, filled with anticipation, preparation, and prayer. If both of them bear in mind all along that they are not yet a married couple, their engagement can be pleasant and enjoyable. Doubts and difficulties that arise during an engagement often come about as a result of too many meetings and too many overlong phone conversations between the bride and groom to be. It is preferable for the schedule of their meetings to be established by a third party, just as they were before the engagement. Parents or counselors can take care of this. Also, it is not wise for the young couple to be involved in financial matters in the period before the wedding. This is a sensitive subject, and exposure to it generally leads to undesirable tension and is totally unnecessary.

Certainly, the pair should meet from time to time during their engagement, so that they do not stand under the *chuppah* as two strangers. There is a certain logic, too, in the custom of each of them inviting the other to eat Shabbos meals with his or her family once or twice during the engagement period, to give them a chance to get acquainted with each other's families. If one side or the other should happen to be celebrating a *simchah*, joyous event, during this period, they would have another opportunity to meet. However, spending Shabbos together each week, and making courtesy visits to all members of their extended families, should wait until after the wedding.

Maran HaGaon HaRav Yosef Sholom Elyashiv, *shlita*, was once asked by a student whether he and his fiancé should have long meetings during their engagement. In his answer, Rav Elyashiv mentioned a response by Rav Yisroel Salanter, *zt"l*, with regard to a knife used in *shechitah*, ritual slaughter. Rav Yisroel Salanter said that the knife should be as short as possible, in order to minimize the chances of a flaw that would render it unusable. The shorter the knife, he said, the less room there is for a flaw to appear. Following the same principle, as Rav Elyashiv explained to the young man, it is preferable to shorten the length of meetings during the engagement period rather than let them be long, so that there will be no room for stumbling.

If we accurately assess the importance of the laws of modesty and understand correctly the essential nature of the engagement period, it will be easier for us to internalize the recognition that, during this period, there should be an added emphasis on these laws. An engaged young woman, beginning to understand the differences in the way men and women are made, finds herself in a new situation. There is a man who likes her. This sensation is a new one for her, and fills up her whole being. She needs to remember that she found favor in the eyes of her future husband for her inner qualities and not for the external ones, and that the more modest she is, the more her inner self will shine forth. Our outer shell is only a covering for the true internal self that lies within.

People tend to fantasize about their engagement period. Young girls imagine how they'll feel walking down the street together with their groom-to-be, and picture this as the height of happiness. In reality, getting engaged only means that a girl is bound to someone for the purpose of marriage. She is a future bride and will soon be a married woman. The engagement period is nothing more than a countdown to the big day.

Girls may not know how to behave during the engagement period, simply because they are unaware of the true essence of marriage. This should be explained to them immediately after they become engaged.

Another important point which should be clarified is that there is no reason for engaged friends to compare the gifts they've received or to pass pictures around among themselves. This is no competition, with the winner being the girl who received the most expensive ring or the shiniest bracelet. How much more should a girl remember that her future husband—and, for a boy, his future wife—is not an appropriate topic of conversation in company. For one thing, it may arouse jealousy; for another, it is a breakdown of the future privacy of their relationship. Privacy is the symbol of the Jewish home. When *bnei Yisrael*, the Jewish people, built their tents in the desert, they were praised for never lining up the entrances facing one another (Rashi on Bamidbar 24:5).

Building a home is an internal labor, and the preparation begins during the engagement period. Both bride and groom to be must be educated in the laws of *taharat hamishpachah* and the ways to build a strong foundation for their future home together. These are the most important preparations of all during the engagement period, and they should not be pushed aside in favor of other matters that one may feel are more important or more pressing. An engaged couple who conduct their engagement period in the correct and proper way, and who use the time to prepare for their married life together, will be thankful for this for the rest of their lives—because they will approach their marriage with all the tools necessary for them to build their own miniature sanctuary.

What engaged couple would not want to prepare properly to build their home—a faithful Jewish home in which the *Shechinah*, the Divine Presence, will rest forevermore?

Chapter 14

The Laws of Modesty

A Woman's Behavior in the Presence of Men

Written by HaGaon HaRav Yitzchak Zilberstein, *shlita*, and approved by Maran HaGaon Rabbi Yosef Sholom Elyashiv, *shlita*

- All the hair on a married woman's head must be covered in all situations.

  If she wears a *sheitel,* wig—the *sheitel* must look like a wig. It must be styled modestly and must not be longer than the highest vertebra on the back.

  In the view of Maran HaGaon Rabbi Yosef Sholom Elyashiv, *shlita*, it is preferable to cover one's hair with a kerchief rather than with a wig.

- The woman's whole body must be covered in all situations.
  - This includes the elbows, knees, collarbone, and the first vertebra on the back.
  - The clothes may not be see-through or tight-fitting.
  - Red clothes or clothes with a slit—are not permitted.

- The woman must wear stockings.
- Makeup and jewelry—should not be prominent.
- Perfume—should not be noticeable.
- The woman must make sure that her voice when singing should not be heard.
- The woman's appearance and behavior should be dignified but not attention-getting.
- The woman must make sure to observe all the laws of *yichud*.

"Nearly all of a woman's reward and punishment in the World to Come are dependent on *modesty" (The Peleh Yoetz, in Chesed La'alafim)*

Yosef Sholom Elyashiv
Jerusalem

BS"D Tishrei 5771

Many have already spoken out about the obligation to strengthen and observe the strictures of modesty in dress, something that is the foundation of the Jewish home and the foundation of the nation as a whole.

And I have already publically stated my opinion that the laws of modesty formulated by the Beis Din "Mishmar HaTorah," which was established by me, are neither fences nor stringencies, but rather they are part of the body of Torah law, and that anyone who detracts from them is transgressing *Das Yehudis*.

The obligation to observe and keep these laws is not incumbent only on the women. Rather, the head of every house in his home must make sure to strengthen the members of his household and his offspring.

Particularly in these days, the days of judgment and mercy, when every individual wishes to be judged favorably, there is no defense on the Day of Judgment like strengthening oneself in these matters, which offers protection against all troubles.

In this merit, may the *Shechinah* rest upon you, and may you merit a *g'mar chasimah tovah* in the book of the righteous.

With the blessing of the Torah,

Yosef Sholom Elyashiv   Aharon Yehuda Leib Shteinman   Shemuel Halevi Wosner

Beth Din Tzedek
Mishmar
Hatorah
Under the leadership of Maranan Verabanan,
the Gedolei Hador shlita,
Maran Hagaon Rabbi Yosef Shalom Elyashiv shlita
and Maran Hagaon Rabbi Shemuel Halevi Wosner shlita
ככל אשר יורוך
AS THEY INSTRUCT YOU

Krias Kodesh

From the *Gedolei Hador shlita*

Tznius and the sanctity of the Jewish People have always been of the fundamental principles of our Nation, and it is these traits that have highlighted the difference between us and the nations of the world. Throughout the generations our ancestors were prepared to give up their lives to guard the principles of *tznius* and to uphold these fortresses of our religion.

Indeed, in places where the barriers of *tznius* were breached, those communities disappeared and no remnant of them remains. It is thus incumbent upon us to separate and distance ourselves from the ways of the *goyim* and from the immoral influences of the outside world.

It is heartening to see that there has recently been a great hisorerus in strengthening the observance of these principles of tznius and the sanctity of the Jewish People, both in our educational institutions as well as among the public at large.

For this purpose a special *Beth Din* in these matters has been established

Beth Din "Mishmar Hatorah"

comprised of the following Rabbonim shlita:

Rabbi Ezriel Auerbach   Rabbi Yisrael Gans

Rabbi Shamai Hakohen Gross   Rabbi Shemuel David Hakohen Gross

Rabbi Yitzchak Darzi   Rabbi Naftali Nussbaum   Rabbi Yehudah Silman

Rabbi Moshe Shaul Klein   Rabbi Chayim Szmerler   Rabbi Baruch Shraga

who have been charged with supervising and encouraging the strengthening and reinforcement of the principles of tznius in all areas, and they have instituted clear rules with regard to the correct form of behavior in these matters according to the Torah.

We therefore take this opportunity to express our wholehearted backing for the aforementioned Rabbonim, the members of the Beth Din, in their tremendous efforts to rectify the breaches in these areas. They are thereby restoring the observance of these laws to their correct level, and the rules they have laid down are the Torah principles for strengthening the regulations and customs that are practiced by all the different sects of our People, according to the tradition handed down to us by our ancestors.

We conclude with a blessing that in the merit of strengthening the observance of Torah and mitzvos and the foundations of the sanctity of the Jewish Nation, may we all be saved from any evil, and be privileged that the Divine Presence rest among the Jewish People and that the Holy Temple be rebuilt, with the coming of Moshiach, speedily in our days.

Yosef Shalom Elyashiv | **Shemuel Halevi Wosner**

Aharon Yehudah Leib Steinman | **Ya'akov Aryeh Alter** (Admor of Gur)

Hak' Yissachar Dov (Admor of Belz) | **Michel Yehudah Lefkowitz**

Avraham Ya'akov (Admor of Sadigura) | **Nissim Karelitz**

Hak' Tzvi Elimelech (Admor of Tzanz) | **Chayim Kanievsky**

Shemuel Auerbach | **Yisrael Hager** (son of the Admor of Vishnitz *shlita*)

I also adjoin my signature – **Hak' Yochanan Sofer** (Admor of Erlau)

HEAD COVERINGS

Halachah requires the covering of all hair on the head. Whichever head covering is used – *sheitel, tiechel* or hat – it must cover all the hair on the head.

THOSE WHO WEAR A *SHEITEL* MUST BE PARTICULAR THAT:

1) They do not appear to be unmarried. It should be clearly recognizable to all that she is a married woman. One must therefore avoid any feature whose purpose is to give the sheitel a natural look. e.g.:
   - a white parting or 'skin top' – scalp colored net
   - a girlish style
2) The sheitel should not have a wild look or be long (The *Gedolei Hador* have described this as *pritzus*). The maximum permitted length is:
   At the back – no longer than just covering the neck;
   At the sides – under no circumstances should it pass the shoulder line;
   At the front – the hair should not cover the cheeks.

THOSE WHO WEAR A *TIECHEL* SHOULD BE CAREFUL OF THE FOLLOWING PITFALLS:

1) 'Bandana' tiechels are generally not large enough to cover all the hair as is required by halachah.
2) Some hats are not sufficiently opaque and therefore do not provide proper coverage of the hair as is required by halachah (e.g. an unlined net fabric).
3) Long snoods may get pulled backwards because of their own weight and thereby reveal the hair at the front of the head.
4) When a snood or tiechel is worn above the ears, the hair around the ears is visible.

DRESS

BLOUSES – TOPS

The neck itself is considered an exposed area that need not be covered.

The boundaries of the neck are as follows:

- At the sides – from the point where the shoulders begin to slope downwards.
- From behind – from the first bone of the spine (a necklace will naturally hang at this point).
- In front – from just above the collarbone. (In certain situations, such as when carrying a shoulder bag or lifting an infant, the sides of the neck can become exposed. Leaving the top button open on a shirt collar can cause exposure at the front).

LENGTH OF THE BLOUSE

It must be long enough that the body is not exposed in any position, even if one is wearing another garment underneath (i.e. at least 10 cm past the waist).

SLEEVE LENGTH AND SHAPE

It should be long enough that the elbow is covered in all positions. One may not wear a garment with tight fitting sleeves.

SHAPE OF BLOUSE

A tight-fitting blouse is forbidden. Therefore, fabrics that cling to the body (such as lycra or t-shirt material) are forbidden to be worn, even when worn under a jacket or vest (waistcoat).

One should not wear a short-sleeved blouse on top of a long-sleeved one.

SIZE OF BLOUSE

One cannot rely on the size printed on the garment label – one must try on the garment and ensure that it is not too tight.

SKIRTS

Skirts may not be shorter than halfway between the knee and the heel.

The style must be wide enough that the shape of the legs will not show when walking.

Position – the top of the skirt should begin at the waist – not above or below.

Slits are forbidden, even below the knee.

STOCKINGS

Length – the stockings must be at least higher than the knee.

Thickness – that the leg is not visible. (The definition of 'at least 40 denier' does not necessarily hold true, since some manufacturers use a finer thread, meaning that 40 denier will be inadequate, and one must therefore check that the leg is not visible.)

Beth Din Tzedek
Mishmar Hatorah

To *Acheinu Bnei Yisrael*
Around the World

We have been requested by the *Gedolei Hador* to awaken the hearts of *Klal Yisrael* with regard to the conduct of the Jewish household in all aspects.

In our generation, as opposed to earlier generations, many barriers have been breached, especially in the area of *tzniusdik* dress.

In the past, this *mesorah* was transmitted from mother to daughter with no need for elaboration or clarification – these matters were self-understood. In our times, however, things have changed, and to our dismay many external influences have penetrated into even the best homes.

We therefore see a need, as the emissaries of the *Gedolim*, to turn to the head of every household concerning the topic of modest conduct in their Jewish lifestyle and in particular in the subject of dress.

Attached to this letter is a detailed list of regulations and requirements. We hope these words will be taken to heart, strengthen the foundations of Jewish homes and contribute to elevate the glory of the Torah.

We conclude with a *berachah* to all Klal Yisrael – that Hashem may bless them to see their sons and daughters and future generations following the right path, and may *Hakadosh Baruch Hu* fulfill all their heart's desires for the good.

With our sincerest blessings,

Ezriel Auerbach | Yisroel Gans | Shamai Hakohen Gross | Shemuel David Gross
Yitzchak Darzi | Naftali Nussbaum | Yehudah Silman | Moshe Shaul Klein
Chayim Szmerler | Baruch Shraga

Every Jewish girl is obliged to wear garments in the style of a kosher *Bas Yisroel*, and she must distance herself totally from the ever-changing fashions of the street, which are considered unacceptable. About this it says:

הולך את חכמים יחכם רועה כסילים ירוע

"One who follows the wise will become wise, but one who is drawn after fools will find evil."

Educators who are entrusted with the chinuch of our girls must establish what is 'street-wear,' from which one must keep far away.

Kehillos that have accepted upon themselves further standards of tznius, e.g. they do not wear any type of sheitel, but only a hat or tiechel, or those who are accustomed to wearing a hat or tiechel on top of their sheitels, a closed collar that covers the neck, sleeves that extend to the wrist, etc., are required to uphold these customs and may not change these minhagim. About this it says: אל תטוש תורת אמך "Do not forsake the teaching of your mother."

P.O.B. 57768, Jerusalem, ISRAEL Tel. 972-50-4166547

Summary of the Laws of Modesty

Written by Beth Din Tzedek "Mishmar HaTorah,"
Under the leadership of Maranan Verabanan,
the Gedolei Hador shlita,
Maran Hagaon Rabbi Yosef Shalom Elyashiv shlita,
and Maran Hagaon Rabbi Shemuel Halevi Wosner shlita.

Head Coverings

Halachah requires the covering of all hair on the head. Whichever head covering is used—sheitel [wig], tiechel [kerchief] or hat—it must cover all the hair on the head.

Those who wear a sheitel [wig] must be particular that:

1) They do not appear to be unmarried. It should be clearly recognizable to all that she is a married woman. One must therefore avoid any feature whose purpose is to give the sheitel a natural look.

   e.g.:

   - a white parting or "skin top"—scalp-colored net
   - a girlish style

2) The sheitel should not have a wild look or be long. (The *Gedolei Hador* have described this as *pritzus*). The maximum permitted length is:

   - At the back—no longer than just covering the neck; and under no circumstances should it pass the shoulder line;
   - At the front—the hair should not cover the cheeks.

Those who wear a tiechel [kerchief] should be careful of the following pitfalls:

1) "Bandana" tiechels are generally not large enough to cover all the hair as is required by halachah.
2) Some hats are not sufficiently opaque, and therefore do not provide proper coverage of the hair as is required by halachah (e.g., an unlined net fabric).
3) Long snoods may get pulled backwards because of their own weight and thereby reveal the hair at the front of the head.
4) When a snood or tiechel is worn above the ears, the hair around the ears is visible.

Dress

Blouses-Tops

The neck itself is considered an exposed area that need not be covered.

The boundaries of the neck are as follows:

- At the sides—from the point where the shoulders begin to slope downwards.
- From behind—from the first bone of the spine (a necklace will naturally hang at this point).
- In front—from just above the collarbone. (In certain situations, such as when carrying a shoulder bag or lifting an infant, the sides of the neck can become exposed. Leaving the top button open on a shirt collar can cause exposure at the front.)

Length of the Blouse

It must be long enough so that the body is not exposed in any position, even if one is wearing another garment underneath (i.e. at least 10 cm. past the waist).

Sleeve Length and Shape

It should be long enough that the elbow is covered in all positions. One may not wear a garment with tight-fitting sleeves.

Shape of Blouse

A tight-fitting blouse is forbidden. Therefore, fabrics that cling to the body (such as lycra or t-shirt material) are forbidden to be worn, even when worn under a jacket or vest (waistcoat).

One should not wear a short-sleeved blouse on top of a long-sleeved one.

Size of Blouse

One cannot rely on the size printed on the garment label—one must try on the garment and ensure that it is not too tight.

Skirts

Skirts may not be shorter than halfway between the knee and the heel.

The style must be wide enough so that the shape of the legs will not show when walking.

Position—the top of the skirt should begin at the waist—not above or below.

Slits are forbidden, even below the knee.

Stockings

Length—the stockings must be at least higher than the knee.

Thickness—that the leg is not visible. (The definition of 'at least 40 denier' does not necessarily hold true, since some manufacturers use a finer thread, meaning that 40 denier will be inadequate, and one must therefore check that the leg is not visible.)

BS"D 4 MarCheshvan 5772

A Message from Rabbeinu HaGaon Rav Chaim Kanievsky, *shlita*:

"Because the matter of modesty is the foundation of the soul of the Jewish people, and the Rebbetzin, *a"h*, devoted her life to it, it is certainly warranted, and will be an elevation for her pure soul, to strengthen this matter.

And specifically, by following the guidelines set by the Beis Din 'Mishmar HaTorah,'

which was established and is maintained under the leadership of the *gedolei Yisrael, shlita*, my esteemed teacher and father-in-law, Maran HaGaon Rav Y. S. Elyashiv, *shlita*, and Maran HaGaon Rav S. Wosner, *shlita*. And those who have begun teaching the laws of modesty in educational institutions have done a good thing, and the Rebbetzin, *a"h*, will certainly be a *melitzas yosher* for all those who strengthen themselves in this matter, that they may merit much *nachas* and *siyata d'shmaya*, in this world and in the world to come."

Everything That They Will Instruct You

"You shall be careful to do according to everything that they will instruct you.... You shall not deviate from the word that they will tell you, right and left" (Devarim 17:10–11).

The Ramban explains: "Even if you think in your heart that they are mistaken, and the matter seems as simple to you as the way you know your right from your left, do as they command.... For you must think that they are telling you that your right is 'right', for Hashem's spirit is on those who serve Him and He will not desert his pious ones, so that they will always be protected against errors and stumbling blocks. In the words of the *Sifri* (Shoftim 154): Even if they show you that your right is your left, and your left is your right, you must listen to them."

A young girl from a religious home abandoned her observance of Torah and mitzvos, r"l. One Friday, she packed her things and walked out of the house. Her shattered parents hurried to the home of their rav, Rabbi Moshe Avraham Brozovzky, zt"l, and asked him what to do.

"Is there still a mitzvah that she is connected to?" he asked compassionately.

"Yes," replied the mother. "Up till now, she has not abandoned the mitzvah of modesty. She is very attached to those laws."

"Go home and light the Shabbos candles with a wick

made from a thread from an article of her clothing," the rav said. "And may you have a Good Shabbos."

The mother did as the rav had instructed. She lit the Shabbos candles using wicks that she fashioned from her daughter's clothing.

Late on motza'ei Shabbos, they heard a knock at the door.

"I've come home," their daughter said simply from the doorway. "On Friday night, something happened to me. I don't know what. I can't explain it... but I've come home for good."

"When a woman is careful and particular in her observance of the mitzvah of modesty, according to the law, and because of this, beads of perspiration appear on her forehead. *HaKadosh Baruch Hu* takes these drops and keeps them in His treasure-house. And in the next world, these will turn into dewdrops, which will revive her at the Resurrection of the Dead and the life of the World to Come. And she is rewarded for eternity—forever and ever."

(Brought in the name of the Chazon Ish, in Pe'er Hador)

This is the power of the mitzvah of modesty—what Jewish woman would forgo the help from Heaven that comes with it?

Chapter 15

A G-d-Fearing Woman, She Shall Be Praised

Several days before Shuki Malul passed away from the world, the city's chief rabbi came to see him. The rabbi was emotional, and tears flowed from his eyes.

"I envy you, Shuki," he said. "You are going up to Heaven with so many merits and good deeds!"

Shuki was known throughout the northern city in which he lived for his broad range of activities for the community—without any thought of reward. He supported innumerable families and had overseen the establishment of industrial concerns in the city in order to provide its residents with occupations and livelihoods; he helped many people obtain interest-free loans so they could get on their feet; and, on Fridays, he would arrange to have food parcels delivered to the needy.

Shuki had worked tirelessly with the mayor's office to have a religious school opened in the city; he'd enlisted the aid of good Jews to renovate the synagogue; he'd opened a girls' school, kindergartens, nightly yeshivah programs for teenage boys, and a kollel where young married men could learn Torah.

From morning to night, he toiled on behalf of needy families and people in difficult circumstances. When someone required a complicated surgery abroad, it was Shuki who made sure to obtain the necessary funds; when a widow couldn't pay her mortgage and the bank threatened to evict her from her apartment, again it was Shuki who met with the bank manager to work out a reasonable payment schedule.

When the soldier son of one of the city's families was killed in an encounter with terrorists, Shuki immediately came to the family's assistance, helping in any way he could to arrange the funeral and the shivah. For thirty years, Shuki had been a familiar and beloved figure around town, as he raced around on the public's behalf and helped people in any way that he could.

Even during his illness, Shuki's activities did not stop. He persuaded shopkeepers in the city's commercial center to obtain kosher certification from the local rabbinate, he managed to obtain a donation for the construction of a kosher mikveh in a remote neighborhood, and he continued to help people who had fallen into debt.

Now, as he lay on his deathbed, Shuki wished to tell the rabbi his life story. "It would be worthwhile to publicize this," he said, "so that people will realize the significance of every small act.

"I was born into a family that was distant from Judaism,

and until I was twenty I had no idea what Torah and mitzvot were. One day, I was sitting on the street corner with my friends, drinking beer and laughing at the whole world. Across the street was an advertising poster with an immodest picture on it. From where we sat, we could see a religious youth coming up the street. Suddenly, he saw the picture on the poster. Quick as a flash, he averted his head and ran until he was far away from the place. The whole gang was rolling with laughter, but it made me stop and think.

" 'That boy managed to control himself and not look at the picture,' I thought to myself. 'Apparently, he has something better in his life. I'd better check out what it is.'

"I couldn't stop thinking about the matter. It disturbed my peace of mind. I began investigating and asking questions, until I merited to discover the light of Torah. And that's how I got to where I got.

"I don't know who he was, that religious youth who ran away from the immodest picture. I never met him again. But everything that I've done in my life, and all the merits that I've accrued—all of it is in his merit and in the merit of that one act of his. An act that led me to repentence."

"It would be worthwhile to publicize this story," Shuki concluded, "so that people will realize that every action of theirs can have far-reaching ramifications for the good—or, Heaven forbid, for the bad. Woe unto a person who causes others to sin, and fortunate is he who causes others to merit blessing."

(As told by Rabbi Dovid Kleiner, from the Shalom La'Am Center)

"It is a time of trouble for Yaakov." These are difficult times for the Jewish people. Torah study flourishes as never before and a thirst for spiritual growth has become widespread to an extent utterly unparalleled in our history— but despite this, we are witnessing phenomena that threaten our very existence. Eretz Yisrael faces a prolonged and constant threat of annihilation; huge portions of our nation, the world over, are vanishing through pervasive assimilation; people of all ages are dying of strange and terrible diseases; a section of the general public is nurturing a blind hatred for the Torah-observant population, especially in Israel; and there are those, raised in good, G-d-fearing homes, who are abandoning their observance of Torah and mitzvos and have gone out, figuratively, to graze in foreign fields.

With the knowledge that whatever happens in the world is meant to teach us a lesson, it is fitting that we also take a look at the state of the world at present. In this restless period in which we live, the whole world is in a state of upheaval. Whole countries have suffered, and continue to suffer, from earthquakes, floods, tsunamis, and other natural disasters. The world is also suffering from man-made calamities such as war, terror, crime, and severe financial crisis.

All of this is taking place despite the increased growth of Torah study in our generation, and despite the increasing investment in spiritual growth that characterizes our age. HaGaon Rabbi Aharon Yehuda Leib Shteinman, *shlita*, explains that the reality that we are experiencing is the actualization of the Torah's words, "So that He will not see a shameful thing among you and turn away from you" (Devarim 23:15):

"This is the reality of [the words] "and turn away from you," and it is a very serious thing. People in such situations seek all sorts of *segulos*, spiritual remedies, in order to stop the troubles, but we have to realize that we must strengthen ourselves very much in the area of modesty, so that "He will not see a shameful thing among you and turn away from you." As when that happens, G-d forbid, all sorts of troubles are liable to occur. Strengthening our modesty has the power to put a halt to the continuation of this terrible situation."

We, who have merited living in this special generation of "*ikvasa d'Meshicha*"—the footsteps of the Mashiach—must strengthen ourselves with faith in the One Above, with holiness and with unity, all of which are linked to one another.

Our Sages tell us that all the travails that Yosef Hatzaddik experienced will be visited on Zion (*Tanchuma*, *Vayigash* 10); [the numerical value of "Yosef" and "Zion" are the same: 156]. Just as Yosef faced three tests—connected to faith in G-d, holiness, and unity—so, too, must our generation face these three tests.

The more women succeed in recognizing that they were created by G-d and in His image, and that He watches over them and directs them, the higher their spiritual level will be. Their closeness to their Creator will turn their understanding of their feminine essence into something almost natural for them. This awareness will help them safeguard their feminine essence and give it expression in the right place: in their home. Then they, themselves, will seek out ways to fortify their walls of protection.

"You are children to Hashem, your G-d" (Devarim 14:1). Jewish women are the daughters of Hashem. He is the one who imbued them with nobility as a part of their very essence.

Jewish princesses conduct themselves with nobility and respectability. Their clothes are not provocative or seductive, because such things are completely opposed to nobility. Their royal title demands that they refrain from any behavior that borders on the coarse. Their entire being is an embodiment of *kiddush Hashem*—the sanctification of G-d's Name—and this expresses itself in conduct that is refined, simple, and pleasant. This kind of respectable behavior allows them to conceal all inner glory deep within them. And that is their deep, innermost, and truest essence.

When the Queen of Sheba came to Yerushalayim to meet King Shlomo, she brought with her 6,000 identical boys and girls, in order to test his wisdom and see if he could distinguish the boys from the girls. King Shlomo watched the children as the servants served them food. Immediately he saw that some of them lifted their garments to hold the food, while others behaved more modestly. He immediately concluded that the more modest children were girls—and he was correct. The clear knowledge that modesty is embedded deep within the essence of every Jewish girl and woman is what led King Shlomo to solve the riddle.

Women were born to be modest. It comes naturally to them. It is not hard to be what G-d intended us to be: His princesses. Because this is His will, he provides Heavenly assistance to his daughters. He helps them to conduct themselves like royalty. This is especially true in these times of *ikvasa d'Meshicha*, when so many trials lay in wait to ambush us. As Rabbi Eliyahu Lopian, *zt"l*, said, when the war between holiness and impurity is at its peak and the decisive moment is approaching, both sides invest all the effort at their disposal. Who will win? In times like these, a person's smallest action could be the deciding factor. Rabbi Shlomo Zalman Auerbach, *zt"l*, said that every tiny improvement in the area of modesty has a value and a significance that our minds cannot encompass. The reward that awaits a modest woman is immeasurable—both in this world and the next.

Despite some misgivings, Shira's curiosity had gotten the better of her. She was on her way to visit her friend, Noah, who had recently married after becoming Torah- and mitzvah-observant. Keeping the mitzvos was certainly not for her, she thought, but she was interested in seeing, up close, how her friend Noah was living these days. That was why she had accepted her friend's invitation to spend Shabbos at her home. After all, she had no other plans for the weekend....

Late Friday afternoon, Noah lit the Shabbos candles and asked Shira if she wanted to accompany them to shul. Shira had never, ever set foot in a shul. It ought to be an interesting experience, she thought. Why not?

"I'll lend you some of my own more suitable clothes," Noah offered. She pulled a modest blouse and skirt from her closet and handed them to Shira.

Shira looked at the clothes with disfavor. The very suggestion that she wear them felt insulting. She pictured the way she'd look in them, and the image did not please her. What was wrong with her own clothes? Finally—only to avoid hurting her friend's feelings—she put them on.

To her surprise, she didn't look so bad. Strangely, she felt as if the clothing enveloped her in a kind of inner glow. "Just like the light of the candles," she said to herself.

Shira was transfixed by the lovely tunes of the prayers she heard in the synagogue. The meal that followed the service was simply out of this world. And the rest, as they say, is history.

Today, Shira has a mitzvah-observant family of her own. When she thinks back to her transformation from secular young girl to G-d-fearing homemaker raising her children to Torah and mitzvos, she can't help shaking her head with wonder as she remembers how it all began with those modest clothes.

The laws of modesty increase holiness in the world. Keeping

them is an expression of fear of Heaven—and faith in G-d. We are all called upon to unite around the challenge of keeping the Torah's laws. These are the trials that the Jewish people must face at the end of the days, and they are all within our reach. All we must do is strengthen our belief in our ability to overcome the obstacles and bring about the longed-for Redemption.

Every day, we pray, "May our eyes behold Your return to Zion in compassion." In his work *Ye'aros Devash*, Rav Yonasan Eibishitz, *zt"l*, says, "When a person says, 'May our eyes behold', one should have in mind that this should come about through one's own merit—for whatever comes about through one's merit, one will be able to see, but what comes through the merit of one's forefathers, one cannot see…Therefore, *HaKadosh Baruch Hu* promised that, in the future, the people of Israel will be redeemed in their own merit. And that is why we request, 'May our eyes behold.'"

The women of our generation have a special mission, as outlined by Maran HaGaon Rav Yosef Sholom Elyashiv, *shlita*, in no uncertain terms: "If we repair the matter of modesty, there will be peace." This is because the main war of impurity with holiness is taking place today in the arena of immorality, and it is this impurity which distorts our faith.

Women have the power to increase holiness. "In the merit of the righteous women who lived in that generation, Israel was redeemed from Egypt" (*Sotah* 11b). As it happened in the past, so may it take place again in the future, as the *Midrash Zutah Ruth* (4:11) says: "The generations will be redeemed only through the merit of the generation's righteous women." Therefore women who safeguard their modesty are helping to bring the Redemption closer (*Kav Hayashar*, ch. 82).

Rebbetzin Bas-Sheva Kanievsky, *a"h*, told a story that highlights the power of modesty:

One day, a woman came to see me, her mode of dress and

speech testifying to her distance from mitzvah observance. With great difficulty, a relative had persuaded her to come to talk to me despite her deep hostility to every expression of Judaism.

In the midst of our conversation, my seven-year-old granddaughter walked into the room crying. I tried to find out what was troubling her, but she was sobbing so hard that it was difficult for her to speak. Finally, between one sob and another, she managed to tell me that she was crying because a button had fallen off her blouse. How could she walk around this way? It wasn't modest!

It wasn't until I'd located a safety pin and fastened it on her blouse in place of the missing button that she calmed down and went away, a smile on her face.

At that moment, the woman sitting with me burst into tears. She, too, began sobbing uncontrollably. The innocent faith of that seven-year-old girl, and her concern for observing the laws of the Torah, had profoundly touched my guest's heart. And from that day on, she resolved to move gradually closer to Hashem; and, as a first step, she decided to start improving her dress.

Today, she is a mitzvah-observant woman, scrupulous about all the Torah's laws—but she will always have a special place in her heart for the mitzvah of modesty. This was the mitzvah that provided the tiny opening through which she began moving closer to her Creator. As the Midrash says: "My children, make me a tiny opening of repentance, like the eye of a needle—and I will make openings that wagons and carriages might pass through!" (Shir HaShirim Rabbah 5:3).

In the final analysis, modesty is a matter of *yiras Shamayim*—fear of Heaven. G-d instructed His daughters to dress in clothing that provides them with a becoming covering. We faithfully fulfill this command, in simple faith: If this is what G-d wants of us, then this is what we'll do! Of course, it becomes easier for us to properly observe this commandment when we understand, at least to some degree, the reasons and the myriad benefits bound up in it. But even without a deep understanding, we carry out the will of our Creator without hesitation. This is our greatness. As King Shlomo said: "A G-d-fearing woman—she shall be praised!" (Mishlei 31:30)

Royal princesses have the ability to hasten the Redemption—literally. When we plead before the King of kings to "shine a new light on Zion, and may we all soon merit to bask in its light," and when we beg G-d to "send the Mashiach, at the end of days, to redeem those who eagerly await His salvation," we must know that any effort we make toward self-improvement can be decisive and have an influence on the entire world—until at last we see the fulfillment of the prophecy: "For G-d will comfort Zion, He will comfort all her ruins; He will make her wilderness like Eden and her wasteland like a garden of G-d; joy and gladness will be found there, thanksgiving and the sound of music" (Yeshayahu 51:3).

Does there exist a Jewish woman who would not wish to be the unique princess who hastens the Redemption, speedily in our day?

"There is nothing greater than prayer"

(*Tanchuma, Mikeitz 9*)

A Prayer for the Couple

"May it be Your will, our G-d and the G-d of our forefathers,
that You implant in the heart of Israel, Your nation,
to believe with full faith in the Torah
and in all the words of Your servants, the Sages of Israel.
And they should believe in You and in Your Providence,
and their belief should be constant, and they should not be troubled by troubles of tomorrow,
and they should not be troubled by tribulations of this world.
And they should not become angry and they should not anger You, and they should not forget You.
And they should not remove their thoughts from love and fear of You even for a moment,
and feelings of spiritual arousal and love and fear of You and stirrings of repentance
should be constant and increase within them, without cessation.
And they should cleave to You constantly, and all of their deeds should be for the sake of Heaven."

(Otzar Tefillot Yisrael)

"אין לך גדולה מן התְפִלה"

(תנחומא מקץ, ט)

תפילה לבני הזוג

ויהי רצון מלפניך ה' אלוקינו ואלוקי אבותינו,
שתיטע בלב עמך ישראל
שיהיו מאמינים באמונה שלֵמה בתורה
ובכל דברי עבדיך חכמי ישראל
ויהיו מאמינים בך ובהשגחתך,
ויהיה ביטחונם בך תדיר, ולא יצטערו צרת מחר,
ולא יצטערו על הבלי העולם הזה,
ולא יכעסו ולא יכעיסון ולא ישכחון,
ולא יסירו מחשבתם מאהבתך ויראתך אפילו רגע,
ורשפי התעוררות אהבתך ויראתך והרהורי תשובה
יתמידו ויתרבו בהם בלי הפסק,
ויהיו דבוקים בך תדיר ויהיו כל מעשיהם לשם שמים.

(אוצר תפילות ישראל)

Modesty Enrichment Material

HaGaon HaRav Yitzchak Zilberstein

"So that He will not see a shameful thing among you and turn away from you." (Devarim 23:15)

As we keep seeking the reason behind all the terrible tragedies, we forget the important thing: "So that He will not see a shameful thing among you and turn away from you."

Once, when I came to see my teacher and father-in-law, Maran HaGaon Rav Yosef Sholom Elyashiv, *shlita*, to ask a question and consult with him, I saw a couple who had come for his blessing. The woman was wearing a long wig. After they'd left, R' Elyashiv, *shlita*, expressed his pain over the fact that a lack of modesty prevents blessings from being accepted.

A terrible absurdity is prevalent with regard to modesty. Nearly every day, inspirational gatherings are held to discuss this topic. Respected rabbis and illustrious Torah scholars exert themselves to address the public. And yet, changes in this area are slow in coming!

Clothing and wigs that would have been inconceivable to our forefathers are appearing on our streets, and there is no one to halt the terrible breach that is making inroads even into fine, kosher families—families whose daughters, until just a few years ago, could not have been imagined dressing in such a manner.

We can talk and talk, lecture and lecture; we can hold assemblies for the purpose of strengthening people's resolve throughout the country. But until we understand that modesty is a crown—a veritable crown, studded with sparkling diamonds—the situation will not change.

How troubling it is to witness proof that we've forgotten the simplest thing of all: Modesty is a crown on a woman's head! This is well worth repeating: A crown! An actual crown!

Just so! No exaggeration!

And if we've never seen a queen of any country feel embarrassed by the crown she wears on her head so that she takes it off, yet we see the daughters of Zion taking *their* jewels off, it is a sign that we are completely unaware of the value of modesty.

For if we knew that it is a sparkling crown, we would not remove it with such disdain!

It's All Happening for One Reason: "A Shameful Thing"

Let's talk about the subject of modesty in the simplest possible terms. Let us try to forget, for the moment, everything that we already know or have heard about it, and focus on the verse at the head of this chapter. Let's try to understand what that verse demands of us.

"For Hashem, your G-d, walks in the midst of your camp to rescue you and to deliver your enemies before you; so your camp shall be holy, so that He will not see a shameful thing among you and turn away from you" (Devarim 23:15).

True, we've heard many sermons delivered on this verse, and have read numerous articles on the subject of modesty that expound on the commentaries that have been written about it. But have we ever tried to think seriously about the significance to be found in the simple meaning of the words of the verse? If we were to do so, it is very possible that there would no longer be any need for so many assemblies on the subject of modesty....

What is written here is very simple. If we are afraid to walk the streets of Israel today because of fear of "suicide bombers"; if we tremble to wake up every morning lest we hear another tragic story of a young man cut off in the prime of his life; if we've lost count of the increasing number of orphans, *r"l*; if our hearts skip a beat at every rustling leaf, and from day to day we grow more convinced that we can't go on living this way any longer—we must begin by realizing that all of this is happening because of what the Torah itself labels "*ervas davar*." A "shameful thing."

How does the verse put it? "For Hashem, your G-d, walks in the midst of your camp to rescue you and to deliver your enemies before you." G-d, our merciful Father, wants to rescue us from all of our troubles and to redeem us from all our suffering—on one condition: "Your camp shall be holy." Plain and simple.

Walking in Circles

"So that He will not see a shameful thing among you and turn away from you." In other words, if G-d sees a shameful thing among us, He will turn away from us and won't protect us anymore. And that's when all the troubles begin to come our way, *r"l*.

We try to discover the reasons for all the terrible things that keep happening. We turn here and seek help; we go there and pray for salvation. We're walking in circles, having forgotten the primary thing: "So that He will not see a shameful thing among you and turn away from you."

Is there any more explicit verse that spells things out so clearly for us? If only we'd pause a moment in the race of our lives and try to think about what this verse is telling us, we would "read" the handwriting on the wall and know what to do!

The term *tzniyus*, "modesty," has long since lost its simple meaning. And it *is* simple: not to draw the eye. Not to attract attention. A woman who does not adopt this rule in her approach to modesty has not even begun to fulfill what the Torah demands from her in this area. An area that forms the most basic foundation of the individual Jewish home, and the most basic foundation of the Jewish nation as a whole.

A woman may put on an outfit that covers her body in accordance with the rules, and she may wear a wig that conceals every strand of her hair. But if the clothing or the wig she wears draws attention because they are too tight, too colorful, or for any other reason—she no longer falls into the category of a modest woman. Because, with her own clothing and wig, she is causing men to look at her!

Rav Shlomo Zalman Waited by the Yichud Room

HaGaon R' Reuven Karlenstein tells a powerful story that highlights the enormous error of displaying a lack of caution in these areas.

Decades ago, Maran HaGaon Rav Shlomo Zalman Auerbach, *zt"l*, raised an orphan girl in his home. When she reached marriageable age, he personally undertook to find her a husband who was an outstanding Torah scholar, and brought her to the *chuppah.*

After he'd conducted the marriage ceremony, the guests were astonished to see Rav Shlomo Zalman walk over to the place where the *yichud* room was situated and wait a long time, until bride and groom were ready to emerge.

The situation was so strange that the *yichud* witnesses wondered if Rav Shlomo Zalman was distrustful of their testimony. The parents of the young couple were also mystified. But no one managed to unravel the mystery.

Rav Shlomo Zalman calmed all their fears—but stayed where he was.

Finally, when the door opened and the photographer was about to go in to start taking pictures, Rav Shlomo Zalman asked him to wait outside while he spoke privately to the bride and groom.

The *gaon* walked into the room, closed the door behind him, and wagged a warning finger at the bride. "This is the last time I'm going to see you wearing a wig like that!"

Frightening.

Rav Shlomo Zalman Auerbach, *zt"l*, with all the love for his fellow Jews that bubbled within him, with all the warmth that he showed orphans—to the extent that he, personally, raised that orphan girl in his own home—did not show an understanding and forgiving attitude this time. Upon seeing the bride in a wig that was not modest enough, he scolded her in front of her new husband, and warned her never to wear such a wig again. Rav Shlomo Zalman saw fit to do this in order to educate the orphaned bride that he'd raised, and to help her achieve the way to true happiness and contentment for the rest of her life.

Do We Have Anything to be Ashamed Of?

Ought we be ashamed of our standards of modesty?! What is this embarrassment all about?

The problems already begin at a young age, when girls wear clothes that do not adhere to the rules of modesty, justifying themselves, saying, "Mom, my best friend also wears these kinds of clothes! Why should I be the only one walking around in old-fashioned clothes that aren't in the new style? My cousin wears them, too—and so does my aunt...!"

What is the correct way to respond to this? The answer is very simple: "My daughter, if you saw your best friend or cousin desecrating the Shabbos or eating something unkosher, Heaven forbid—would you then still say, 'But my best friend does it!'?"

That's all. Is there a need for anything more?

Thousands of Thousands of Sins in a Single Moment

There are doubtless many Jewish families that would like to keep the laws of modesty in their entirety, but have never devoted much thought on the question of "What *is* modesty?" As a result, they allow their daughters to dress the way they do.

But when parents sit their daughters down and explain to them—as well as to themselves—that the definition of modesty is not to be eye-catching, then all questions and problems will fall away of their own accord.

The Vilna Gaon writes that, just as Torah study is a man's primary mitzvah, *tzniyus*—modesty—is a woman's primary mitzvah. And just as the evil inclination exerts all its power to distance men from Torah, so too it exerts its full strength to separate women from modesty.

This helps us understand why this is such a challenging area, and how it can be that a woman who is called "religious" may walk down the street and cause thousands of serious sins a minute for the men who look at her.

Great Is the Reward of a Modest Woman!

Rabbeinu Yona, in his *Sha'arei Teshuvah*, writes explicitly that a woman must dress in such a way that people will not look at her. And yet, today, all thought is given to the vexing problem of, "How can I get people to look at me more?"!

How terrible—where have we come to? We've lost touch with all of our principles....

The Gemara (*Berachos* 24a) says, "Whoever gazes at [even] the little finger of a woman—even if he has Torah [scholarship] as great as Moshe Rabbeinu, he will not be spared the judgment of Gehinnom." What can we say to that?

Here's the bottom line: We must sit down with our daughters and explain to them, in detail, about the enormity of a modest woman's reward, and the great merit that will accrue to her in the world of truth—on the one hand. And, on the other, of the terrible angels of destruction, *r"l*, that are destined to greet the immodest woman, who not only sinned but also caused others to sin.

"Don't envy them," parents should tell their daughters, when the girls cite, as proof, their friends who don't dress in accordance with the guidelines of modesty.

She's Surprised That He Went Astray?

The situation has reached such a level of absurdity that people don't even realize what they're doing.

HaGaon Rabbi Yehuda Ades, *rosh yeshivah* of the Kol Yaakov Yeshivah, relates that he is frequently visited by parents who speak with great sorrow about their son who has gone astray, left yeshivah, and embraced an improper lifestyle. They beg the *rosh yeshivah* for advice as to what to do and how to behave with their son.

"I look at those parents," Rabbi Ades continues. "Usually, the father is a *ben Torah* and the mother was educated in Bais Yaakov. And I am shocked by what my eyes see. The mother of the boy in question is not dressed in accordance with the rules of modesty. And then she wonders what went wrong! She expresses surprise that her son left the correct path? Amazing! How could the son *not* turn to sin? Did he have anyone to teach him the path of *mussar*, self-improvement?"

As we've said, in all the talk about modesty we may have lost our sense of proportion. If we've reached a state where a mother does not connect her son's spiritual deterioration with her own lack of modesty, what can one say to her?

The Chofetz Chaim was once asked whether a certain stringency in the area of modesty should be observed. He replied that because the mitzvah of modesty has a direct impact on the state of the Jewish nation as a whole, it is certainly a good thing to behave with stringency wherever possible. After all, every improvement in this area will cause G-d to "walk in the midst of your camp," and every instance of straying from the paths of modesty is liable to bring about a situation in which He will "turn away from you." We can learn from this that every enhancement of the mitzvah of modesty bears a very great significance indeed.

No Comforters Will Succeed in Comforting Him

It is vital to remember that G-d is greatly distressed over every Jewish home that does not conduct itself with modesty. And the greatest distress of all is over the fact that this deterioration has touched Orthodox homes as well.

We can compare this to a father who has seen several of his children abandon and betray him, and have disconnected from him. The father's pain is unimaginable.

But he has one son who's promised never, ever to abandon or betray him. The father takes comfort in that son, and relies on his love.

When that son, too, turns his back on his father and leaves him, it is impossible to describe the father's pain and anguish. Many people may come to try and comfort him, to encourage him—but they will not succeed.

The Main Thing Is Missing from the Book

The situation has reached a point where a woman may hold lengthy discussions with her friend about the importance of modesty—while she herself is dressed in clothing that contradicts everything she's talking about! How is this possible?

Very simple: She does not understand what *tzniyus*, modesty, really is.

As opposed to many other mitzvos, whose observance or, Heaven forbid, non-observance, has nothing to do with those surrounding a person, the area of modesty and its obligations on a woman are inextricably bound up with other people who are necessarily impacted by her modesty or, Heaven forbid, her immodesty. If a woman dresses immodestly, not only does she damage her own honor as a daughter of Israel, but she is also liable to harm many people, causing them to stumble in the area of seeing that which is forbidden, and so on.

The absurdity of it all is heartrending. There are women who are truly righteous, whose every action is for the sake of Heaven, who are building beautiful Jewish homes, enabling their husbands to study Torah, carefully supervising their children lest they set foot in any improper place, and whose faces radiate their fear of Heaven—yet despite all this, some of these same women may be dressed in a way that is the exact opposite of the concept of modesty. We have no choice but to arrive at an inescapable conclusion: They have no clue as to what disturbs the other side, and so they do not know from what and how to guard themselves.

The true definition of modesty is to be modest…not to stand out, to behave in a way that will not attract attention, so that someone can pass her by without being drawn into any thought or action. Even if a woman is wearing a dress of the appropriate halachic length, but it is made of a fabric or is in a color that attracts the eye—she is already acting as a stumbling-block to others.

A modest woman is one who does not draw attention to herself.

The following is another example of the practical lack of awareness in this area. Frequently, women are seen waiting for their husbands outside the synagogue after Shabbos services. They may be standing opposite the shul, or even on the same side as the hundreds of men are coming out. Astonishingly, there are righteous women to whom it would not occur that waiting by the shul at such moments runs contrary to the rules of modesty. And we must ask ourselves: Where is a Jewish woman's natural sensitivity to take care that others do not look at her?

It is as we said earlier. These are truly righteous women. They understand their obligation in the world and we would not, Heaven forbid, wish to say a word against any of them. The problem is an absence of practical awareness about behaving with modesty. Knowing exactly what is permitted and what is forbidden.

The principal of a Torah institution in Jerusalem told me about a girl from the city of Chaleb, Syria, who made her way to Eretz Yisrael with great hardship. After many difficult adventures, she finally set foot in the Holy Land and came to study at his school.

Back in Chaleb, she'd learned about the special qualities of Eretz Yisrael and was determined to find her way there at all cost. She left her parents' home and started for the border. At night, she hid in Syrian pastures; more than once, she came close to losing her life through encounters with Syrian military patrols.

Eventually, she reached the border. She paid local Arabs a fortune to help her across, and finally arrived in Jerusalem. The principal told me that even after many days and nights that the administrators of his school had sat with that girl, they had still not heard all the tales that she had to tell.

The first story that she told, before all the others, revolved around a sermon that the rabbi of the Jewish community in Chaleb had delivered on her last Shabbos in her parents' home. What did the rabbi speak about? Nothing more and nothing less than exhorting the women of his congregation not to stand on the balconies of their homes, which faced the synagogue, at the times when the men were leaving the building after services…

The rabbi of Chaleb's warning applied to women standing on the balconies of their own homes. What about all the women in Israel's religious neighborhoods who wait for their husbands—not on a balcony, but on the pavement, right outside the synagogue?

The *Be'er Moshe*, a book of responsa (part 8, 85:2), states:

It is a grave transgression and a very bad custom for women to stand in front of the synagogue gates after the Mussaf service on Shabbos (or on Friday night) waiting for their husbands or simply chatting in groups. For then the men also emerge from shul, and there is no worse mingling and arousal of the *yetzer hara* than this—and the *yetzer hara* succeeds specifically after the Shabbos prayers.

Lately, women have been doing this in order to show off their clothes, and by doing so are unwittingly harming themselves, their husbands, and their children. They are also causing grievous harm to others. Therefore, it is appropriate to forcefully abolish this practice. A blessing on those congregations that have succeeded in getting rid of this bad and ruinous custom, and may my portion be among their good and beautiful deeds.

Indeed, there are certain congregations which, right from the start, have established that women praying in the women's section leave the synagogue several minutes before the end of services, thereby removing the stumbling-blocks discussed above.

How great will the reward be for the woman who tries to carry out her Creator's will, and navigates her life and all her conduct with modesty. Moreover, the Creator has given woman a great gift, whereby she is able to fulfill His will each and every moment, through modest conduct. The Satmar Rebbe, *zt"l*, interprets the woman's blessing, "for having made me according to His will" as having fashioned me in such a way that I am able to serve Him constantly, to carry out His will at every hour of the day, through my modest clothing and all the other trappings of modesty.

"Hashem, G-d of Heaven...will send His angel before you" (Bereishis 24:7)

Rashi explains: "[Avraham] said to [Eliezer], 'Now He is G-d of the heavens and G-d of the earth, for I have familiarized Him in the mouth of people [I have put people in the habit of mentioning him]. But when he took me from my father's house, He was G-d of the heavens but not G-d of the earth, for those who lived in the world did not recognize Him and His name was not commonly mentioned on earth.'"

What is the significance of "I have familiarized Him in the mouth of people"? Why did Avraham need to emphasize this point? If his goal was to enhance G-d's honor, wouldn't this have the opposite effect—by letting everyone know that, up until now, He was not "G-d of the earth"? And were we to speculate that he said this in order to enhance his own honor—impossible! Could it even enter our minds that this was Avraham's motivation?

We can explain this by referring to the Chasam Sofer, who wrote in his commentary on the Gemara (*Bava Basra* 16b): "A fine gem hung from Avraham Avinu's neck, and every sick person who saw it was immediately cured." The "sick people" mentioned here are those who were spiritually unwell, their symptom being a lack of faith. They were incapable of believing that the lives of the righteous are imbued with happiness, not only in the next world, but in this world as well.

These ill people clung to the heretical belief that the reward for those who walk a righteous path begins only in the World to Come. This is what is meant when Avraham says, "When he took me from my father's house, He was G-d of the heavens but not G-d of the earth." This was the state of affairs until Avraham came along and brought G-d's Divine Presence, the *Shechinah*, down to earth. He demonstrated the fallacy of their belief: When these spiritually ill people saw Avraham's wealth, as symbolized by the "fine gem" that dangled from his neck, they were immediately healed. Now they too knew that the righteous can be wealthy in this world as well—despite the fact that they are prohibited from cheating in business or engaging in fraudulent practices....

When Avraham said, "When he took me from my father's house, He was G-d of the heavens but not G-d of the earth," he was not speaking of G-d's actual presence in the world. He was referring to the defective faith of the "sick ones," who claimed that G-d repays those who are faithful to Him only in the World to Come.

A Beloved Mitzvah

This also explains the rest of the verse: "He will send His angel before you, and you will take a wife for my son from there." Avraham said to Eliezer, "Because I have publicized His Name in the world and have brought His Shechinah down to earth, I want my son to do the same. [In the previous Torah portion, we saw that Avraham ordered his children to follow in Hashem's ways, so that Hashem would give Avraham what He'd promised him.] Therefore, please make sure to take a good wife for Yitzchak, for now that I've merited to do this mitzvah, it is dear to me; therefore I would like Yitzchak to continue the tradition—and only if he has a good wife will he be able to fulfill this mission."

We see from here that even a man of Yitzchak's stature, the son of Avraham, our patriarch, would not have attained the exalted heights he reached without a wife like Rivka, who helped him increase the glory of G-d in the world. Only in his wife's merit did he achieve everything that he did.

Modesty Gives Its Adherents Life

Having come this far, it is now time to add that a woman's role in publicizing G-d's Name in the world expresses itself primarily through her trait of modesty. How much has genuine modesty has been distorted in our time—the trait that has been the hallmark of our mothers and grandmothers throughout the ages! As the Creator's faithful servants who are always eager to improve, it behooves us to conduct a thorough and fundamental inner repair job in the area of modesty.

Rabbeinu Yona Gerondi, in his *Iggeres HaTeshuvah* (*se'if* 78), offers the following in his pure language: "A woman must be modest and take care that men do not look at her, apart from her husband. Those who gaze at her face and hands will descend to Gehinnom—and she will be punished along with each and every one of them, because she caused them to sin and did not conduct herself modestly, and they stumbled because of her."

If our streets look the way they do today, it is a sign that we are not truly aware that modesty gives life to those who safeguard it—not only to the woman herself, but to her entire household. The Midrash (*Tanchuma, Vayishlach* 6) tells us: "When a woman is modest in her home, just as the altar atones for all of Israel, so does she atone for her household!"

Is there any further explanation necessary for the terrible tragedies that have beset the Jewish people of late, where individuals of integrity and refinement are leaving us in the prime of their lives? With their deaths, they have commanded us to contemplate our Sages' teaching, which states explicitly that Divine judgment descends on the world because of a lack of observance of the tenets of modesty. Because of all those prestigious and elegant wigs that cause all those who see them to stumble—the exact opposite of

Rabbeinu Yona's words concerning a woman who takes care than men do not look at her!

Raising the Flag!

Know this, Jewish women: If, in walking down a city street, you arouse interest for one reason or another, you can no longer adorn yourselves with the crown of modesty. The beautiful modesty of a kosher Jewish girl expresses itself in one thing, and one thing alone: ***not*** attracting attention.

This is your greatest "medal": to resemble previous generations! To draw close to the way your righteous grandmothers behaved, as they fulfilled their obligation in this world even when walking through the valley of the shadow of death and beset on every side by bitter trials and terrible difficulties. They proudly wore the emblem of Jewish modesty, as befits the daughters of kings!

HaGaon HaKadosh the Divrei Yechezkel of Shinover, eldest son of the Divrei Chaim of Sanz, offers a marvelous explanation of the verse in *Eishes Chayil* (Mishlei 31:14): "She is like a merchant's ships, from afar she brings her sustenance." This would appear to be very puzzling. After all, we are told in no uncertain terms that "the glory of the king's daughter is inward" (Tehillim 45:14). How can she be compared to someone who travels on ships in the course of his business?

The Divrei Yechezkel explains: Every ship sailing the seas has its flag flying from the prow, in order to deter attacks from enemy ships. The analogy of women to "merchant's ships" refers only to the raising of this flag.

If a Jewish woman is interested in safeguarding her modesty, she must raise her flag: She must declare that she is a daughter of our holy fathers Avraham, Yitzchak, and Yaakov, and, as such, completely unconcerned with "what others will say." This modesty will be a safety-anchor for herself and her family against all enemies.

Better for the Feet to Be in the Mud, Than the Eyes...

When HaGaon R' Binyamin Mendelson, *zt"l*, decided to leave the city of Kiryat Atta and move to Komemiyut, he was asked how he could leave a developed city for a settlement that didn't even have paved roads, only mud.

The rav answered: "Better for the feet to be in the mud, than the eyes..."

"Do Not Enter into Temptation"

HaGaon Rabbi Benzion Abba Shaul, *zt"l*, in his *Ohr L'Tzion—Chachmah U'Mussar* (p. 218), writes:

"The best advice is not to enter into temptation at all, especially in the area of holiness, as our Sages have said: 'Theft and immorality, a person desires and covets'(*Makkos* 23b). With regard to these, one must add safeguard on top of safeguard....

"Therefore, one should be careful not to engage in excessive conversation [with a woman], as Yosi ben Yochanan, *ish Yerushalayim*, said: 'Do not converse excessively with a woman.... Consequently, the Sages said: Anyone who converses excessively with a woman causes evil to himself, neglects Torah study, and will eventually inherit Gehinnom'" (*Avos* 1:5).

Isn't It Worth a Few Pennies?

The author of the *Ohr L'Tzion* illustrates this point with an incident. The Kotzker Rebbe once saw a man in a store, bargaining with the female shopkeeper as he tried to get her to give him a discount of a few pennies. Said the Rebbe: "Isn't keeping the dictate of the mishnah, 'Do not converse excessively with a woman,' worth a few pennies to you?"

So That No One Will Come Near Me...

Where are the grand images within whom modesty was once imbued? Where have they gone?

A noted Torah scholar and genuinely pious individual once lived in the Sha'arei Chesed neighborhood of Jerusalem, where he worked in the early-morning hours delivering milk to its residents. The people walking past him at that early hour of the day noticed that the scholar/milkman exuded a foul odor.

Nobody knew what to make of this—until the man himself revealed the source of the smell.

"At this time of day, when I deliver milk, my business is mostly with women. I am afraid of the evil inclination toward immorality. Therefore, each morning, I dip my head in vinegar, which has a bad smell, so that no one will come near me."

That's what modesty among the Jewish people looks like.

I'd like to take this opportunity to mention that the Jewish communities in Turkey had special merits, and that the Ba'al Shem Tov, who once passed through that country, said that he'd met very holy souls there—souls whose holiness paralleled that found in the age of the Tannaim. He remarked that this was all due to the outstanding modesty of the Jewish women in these Turkish communities, who were extremely scrupulous in following the guidelines of modesty.

How to Educate Our Families to the Proper Values

A man once came to Maran HaRav Shach in tears. He said that his wife refused to listen to him, and refused to dress modestly as befit the wife of a ben Torah. Rav Schach asked, "Have you shown her that this pains you? Have you cried over it in front of her?"

If a man wants to educate his family about the value of modesty, he should not cry and complain only when the situation has become intolerable. It is his job to inculcate this value in the home over the course of years, and to introduce an atmosphere of fear of Heaven and Torah observance rather than the pursuit of luxury and the idle pleasures of this world. Of course, he should refrain from bringing unwholesome books or newspapers into the house, and take every precaution to make sure his children do not connect with friends who will drag them down.

We must realize that the war against immodesty does not begin when a problem already exists, and that the main thrust of the battle does not consist of direct talk against the prohibitions in this area. Life should be filled with positive content and a desire to keep the Torah and help others. This will leave no time for negative activities.

The biography of Rabbi Avraham Yaakov HaCohen Pam, *zt"l*, relates the following episode. A woman once called him on a Friday, *erev Shabbos*, to ask about permissible ways to care for her sick baby on Shabbos. The woman sounded almost hysterical. Rav Pam realized that in her current state she would have a hard time understanding his answer, and that the need to alter the usual method of treatment on Shabbos would only increase her sense of stress. In his wisdom, he refrained from giving her a direct answer, and asked instead about her situation and the difficulties facing her.

From what she said, he gathered that the need to care constantly for her sick child had left her little time to prepare for Shabbos, and her anxiety lest she not have everything ready on time was creating a tremendous inner tension. Thinking of some way to help her, he realized that he had a golden opportunity to educate his granddaughter in an act of *chesed*, kindness. The rabbi called his granddaughter and told her to take a friend and go to that woman's home, where they would clean, tidy up, and help with the Shabbos cooking. The girls did as they were told, and returned home filled with satisfaction.

Now, with the house clean and neat and the aroma of good food filling the house, the rabbi called the woman back to ask after the baby's health. Gently, he asked her how she planned to get ready to care for him over Shabbos. This time, the woman sounded much calmer and happier. She was in a frame of mind to absorb his halachic instructions, and ready to do whatever she had to in order to avoid, Heaven forbid, unnecessarily desecrating the Shabbos. The problem was solved even before it had arisen.

Another story in the book revolves around two widows with a mutual newborn grandson. Each of them wanted the baby to be named after her husband. They came to Rav Pam for him to decide.

After he came to the conclusion that it was proper for the child to be named after one of the husbands, Rav Pam called up the other widow. He told her that her husband in Heaven is pleading that his name not become a source of controversy and strife, and has asked that she be given the following message: If she stepped back from her claim, it would be a greater source of merit to him than having the child named after him. The woman accepted this at once, and informed the other grandmother that she was withdrawing her request to use her husband's name. When the other woman heard this, she felt greatly distressed over the fact that *her* husband had merited only having a grandson named after him, and not the larger merit of giving something up for the sake of peace.

Children who are raised in a home in which people are always thinking of others, where everyone helps each other in material ways even in times of stress, will grow up filled with spiritual satisfaction. They will always be looking for the best way to help others, and not seek negative ways to fulfill their needs.

There was once a story about a couple who did not lack for money, but wished to implant in their children's hearts what was important in life. When a son was born to them, they decided not to have the *bris milah* in a fancy hall, but rather in the home of one of the generation's honored Torah leaders. The rav would serve as *sandek* and the members of his *kollel* would all participate in the ceremony. Seeing the simplicity of the rabbi's home, their children would experience, first-hand, how important Torah was to their parents, and would internalize that it is not luxury and ostentation that are primary in life, but the opposite—holiness and the inner essence are paramount.

Along similar lines, the story is told about how Rav Elchonon Wasserman, *zt"l*, explained to his students why a certain prosperous individual had merited marrying his daughters off to Torah scholars, and how he'd educated them to want this. One day, he said, he'd been going around town collecting money for his yeshivah, when he came to that man's house. Rav Elchonon did not wish to enter through the front door because his feet were muddy from the street. Instead, he went around and knocked on the back door.

When the rich man saw who was knocking, he was shaken. In agitation, he asked why the rav had not come to the front door. Rav Elchonon replied that he hadn't wanted to dirty the man's expensive rugs and furniture. In tears, the man begged him to come to the front door, go into the living room and walk on the rugs with all the mud on his feet, so that his daughters, who were accustomed to seeing luxury all the time, would understand that the important thing is not money and costly carpets, but rather honoring the Torah. And so, this man merited sons-in-law who were Torah scholars.

We can learn from all of this that it is our obligation to infuse our homes with a sense of the important things in life: the holy Torah and keeping the mitzvos. Then our children will not look for negative ways to achieve satisfaction in life.

There was once a town that stood on the border between Russia and Poland. In the course of numerous wars between the two countries, the border had been established in the center of the town. The Jewish community, too, was split in two: half on the Russian side, and half on the Polish one.

Each part of the community established institutions to serve its needs—except for the cemetery on the Russian side, which continued to serve both parts. In general, the authorities did not permit crossing the border, but when it came to burying the dead the rules were relaxed. And so, every time someone from the Polish side of the Jewish community died, the residents would obtain a special permit to cross the border, and would conduct the funeral under the watchful gaze of the border police.

One day, someone had an idea. Before setting out for the funeral, he would put a bottle of vodka in his pocket, which he would then sell on the Russian side of the border without having to pay the usual tax. Afterwards, seeing that his scheme had succeeded, his friends decided to expand on it. From then on, everyone who participated in a funeral would bring along a bottle of vodka in every pocket.

With time, when all went well, they decided that there was no need to wait until someone died before using the funeral as an opportunity to smuggle. They would fake a funeral, fill the coffin with dozens of bottles of vodka, and make a huge profit. And so they did.

One day, the border police watching the funeral procession demanded that the coffin be opened so that they could view the body inside. The men in the funeral procession were beside themselves, and begged that the coffin remain sealed so as not to infringe on "the honor of the dead." But the border police did not listen to their importuning, and they approached the coffin with the intention of opening it by force. Then all the participants in that "funeral" began weeping and wailing, because they understood that, in just a moment, the police would discover all the vodka that they'd been attempting to smuggle, resulting in imprisonment of many years for all of them.

The officer in charge told them, "You're too late! Had you wept *during* the funeral, we would not have suspected you, and there would have been no need to weep now. But because there were no tears shed at the funeral, that led us to suspect that you were accompanying something other than a dead body.... And now, there's nothing left for you to do except cry!"

There's a tremendous lesson here for us: In order not to weep in the future, we must pray and cry out to Hashem now, and take pains with our children's upbringing from a very young age. By crying and exerting proper effort while there is still time, we can avoid having to cry in the future.

The Glory of a Princess

We can learn about the importance of modesty, and its essential nature as part of a Jewish woman's character, from various places in our holy Torah. It is worth mentioning here the Tiferes Yisrael's explanation of the seemingly surprising difference between the opening mishnah of the fifth chapter of the Tractate *Shabbos*, and the mishnah that begins the sixth chapter.

The sixth chapter begins as follows: "With what [accessories] may a woman go outside [on Shabbos] and with what [accessories] may she not go out [on Shabbos]?" The mishnah then goes on to list the things that a woman may *not* wear when she goes out into the public domain on Shabbos: "A woman may not go out either with woolen strands or linen strands," etc. The fifth chapter, however, starts with the words, "With what may an animal go out [on Shabbos] and with what may it not go out?"—after which the mishnah goes on to list the things that are permissible for an animal to wear when going into the public domain on Shabbos: "A camel may go out with a halter," etc.

Explains the Tiferes Yisrael: The order was changed, to emphasize the concept of "All the glory of a princess is inward." Therefore, when discussing what women may or may not carry out on Shabbos, the mishnah begins with those things that she is prohibited from taking out.

"For it is your wisdom and discernment in the eyes of the people" (Devarim 4:6)

When HaGaon Rav Shaul Brach, *zt"l*, a Torah luminary from Hungary, was on his way to Eretz Yisrael, he was forced to spend several days in a port city in Greece while waiting for the ship that would take him to the Holy Land.

As destiny would have it, a princess of the British royal family happened to be in the same city at that time. She caught sight of Rav Shaul and his entourage, all of Jewish visage with beard and sidelocks. Deeply impressed by the sight of Rav Shaul's face, she sent one of her escorts to tell the rabbi that she wished to speak with him.

Rav Shaul Brach consented. In the course of their conversation, the British princess raised many questions about the Jewish people and the customs and laws that guide it. The princess said that she, personally, had a high regard for the Jewish religion, and she spoke respectfully and admiringly of the *Tanach*. Rav Shaul Brach answered all of her questions, and it was obvious that she was well satisfied with them.

Near the end of their meeting, the princess asked Rav Brach why it was that, in England, the average citizen had four children at the most, while many Jewish families had ten or even fifteen. The *gaon* replied that the reason for this is found in the family's centrality in Jewish life. As proof, he went on to tell her about the purity and holiness of Israel, and to describe the modesty that characterizes Jewish family life. The princess inclined her head in understanding and said that she was persuaded that this must be so. She parted from Rav Brach, telling him that, for the rest of her life, she would envy the ways of the Jewish nation—and especially its warm and holy family nest.

A Modest Woman Is Beloved of Hashem

The book of Iyov (36:32) says: "He covers the clouds with rain, and commands it upon those who entreat Him." Rashi explains that the clouds will be prevented from sending down rain because of our sins, and the rain will come through those who entreat Him in prayer. Whose prayers are the ones that will be effective in bringing about the rain? "The one who loves his generation; its great and wise one." There are several conditions that a person must meet in order for his prayers to affect his entire generation. One of them is to be "one who loves his generation."

In order for a woman to be one of the generation's beloved individuals, she must conduct herself in a way that is beneficial to her generation—and not, on the contrary, in a manner that harms it. If she dresses modestly, she loves her generation and everyone around her, and both her behavior and her prayers will bring merit to it. If, on the other hand, she does not conduct herself with modesty, she does not love the people of her generation. She is causing them to stumble, so of course her prayers will not be answered by the Creator of the world.

A Woman's Importance in Building and Molding a Jewish Home

We are told in the Torah: "Elazar, son of Aaron, took for himself from the daughters of Putiel as a wife, and she bore to him Pinchas" (Shemos 6:25).

The Netziv, in his *Ha'amek Davar*, comments that the word *lo*, "for himself," seems to be extraneous. In his own words: "It comes to teach us that, although Putiel's daughter was of no greater lineage than Tzipporah, Moshe's wife, she still merited giving birth to Pinchas. This was because she was a great help to Elazar in his life, and because Elazar saw that she helped him become an elevated person he did not care overmuch about her lineage. For this reason she was worthy of being his wife, and of giving birth to a son worthy of him. As it says, 'How do women earn merit? By [sending their] husbands to learn Torah.'"

We see from here how crucial the woman's role is in building and molding the Jewish home. It is her job to help her husband and turn him into an exalted person, and a great deal of her children's success depends on her.

The Gemara (*Bechoros* 60a) states: "Privileged is the mother of Rav Huna bar Sechorah, [who gave birth to such a wise son] who was able to resolve a difficulty in the discourse at the assembly before a festival, in accordance with [his teacher's] own opinion."

Rashi comments: Rav Huna bar Sechorah's mother had the merit of giving birth to a son such as him, who knew how to resolve a difficulty for Rava, his teacher, in the midst of the discourse.

One can ask: Why does the Gemara praise Rav Huna's mother, and not his father, or both his parents?

We see from here that the primary factor for success in raising children is the kind of rearing that the mother provides in the home. That's why the Gemara specifically praises Rav Huna's mother, because it was she who caused him to achieve greatness and to merit Heavenly assistance in his understanding of the Torah.

The general principle is that a great deal depends on the mother's influence. She bears an awesome responsibility, and must raise her children properly. If she conducts herself with the appropriate modesty, she will merit children who possess fear of Heaven and greatness in Torah.

In deep appreciation to
Rabbi Yirmiyohu and Tehilla Abramov

May this work be in memory of our dear mothers

מרת שולמית ב"ר יצחק הלוי קפלן ע"ה
נלב"ע כ"ז באדר שני תשל"ו
ת.נ.צ.ב.ה.
ואמה מרת גענעדע ב"ר שמואל פרוסקוויטס ע"ה
נלב"ע כ"ד בשבט תשי"ט
ת.נ.צ.ב.ה.

מרת יהודית ב"ר ברוך קפלן ע"ה
נלב"ע י"ח בתמוז תשל"ו
ת.נ.צ.ב.ה.

מרת פעסה ב"ר יצחק קיסנר ע"ה
נלב"ע ט' בכסלו תשע"א
ת.נ.צ.ב.ה.
ואמה מרת חיה אסתר ב"ר אביגדור לופיס ע"ה
נלב"ע כ"א בתשרי תש"א
ת.נ.צ.ב.ה.

מרת פייגה ב"ר משה קיסנר ע"ה
נלב"ע כ"ג באדר שני תשד"ם
ת.נ.צ.ב.ה.

Johannesburg, South Africa